the wines of madeira

the wines of madeira

*An indispensable guide to the wines,
grapes and producers*

trevor elliott

Published in 2010 by
Trevor Elliott Publishing
17 Beechcroft Road, Alverstoke, Gosport,
Hampshire PO12 2EP
Telephone: 023 9252 3672
E-mail: *trevorelliottwines@tesco.net*

ISBN: 978-0-9566413-0-4

Designed and printed by:
Studio 6 Design & Print,
The Square, Wickham, Hampshire PO17 5JN
www.studio-6.co.uk

Printed on paper from sustainable sources.

Contents

Foreword

What's the oldest bottle of wine you've ever drunk? If you sniff and spit for a living, it's a question you get asked on a regular basis. I'm fortunate enough to have sampled a couple of red wines from the 1880s and a German Riesling from the 1890s, but the winner by more than half a century was an 1822 Verdelho from Madeira.

This small Portuguese island – humid, volcanic and undeniably atmospheric – is better known as a tourist destination and, to football fans, as the birthplace of Ronaldo, but it's the wines that fascinate me. How does it produce bottles of such complexity (and longevity)? Is it the grape varieties, the soils, the climate, the vinification or the ageing techniques? The answer is that it's a combination of these and other things.

Madeira is an historic wine style, but it's also one that is in danger, partly from developers on an island where land is a valuable commodity, partly from the difficulty of growing grapes on an island with such vertiginous slopes and partly from the ignorance and indifference of consumers. Too many people think that Madeira is something you put in a cake or leave on the dessert trolley; very few are aware that, at its best, it's one of the world's greatest fortified wines.

Trevor's book couldn't be published at a better time. It's well-researched, informative and admirably succinct, covering all aspects of wine production on Madeira, from viticulture to the liquid in the glass, with useful comments on the eight remaining producers and an upbeat chapter about the future of this unique wine. I hope you'll read and enjoy it with a glass of Madeira in hand, preferably one with some bottle age. Anyone for an 1822 Verdelho?

Tim Atkin MW
SUMMER 2010

Introduction and author's acknowledgements

I first tasted Madeira wine, when, more than 20 years ago, I enrolled on a weekend course entitled 'Wine Tasting'. Although it was just a young wine, I can still remember how much I enjoyed it. The intensity, the amazing flavours and the length of time the taste lasted, made me want to try more. Subsequently I took every opportunity to taste more Madeira wines, many of which were delicious. This led to a determination to discover more about them.

When I first visited the island twenty years ago, it was harvest time. I was fascinated to see the boxes of grapes along the roadside, waiting to be taken to the wineries. At one winery, I saw what I thought was a large quantity of Tinta Negra grapes being delivered. When I asked if I was correct, I was guided away from the lorries! It seemed my guide only wanted to talk about the other 4 varieties, which I now know produce only approximately 10% of Madeira wines.

From my studies, Madeira began to stand out as a rather special wine. The 'picture' I built up, was of a fortified wine that could be sweet, medium sweet, medium dry or dry and was made mainly from the 4 grape varieties: Malvasia (sweet); Boal (medium sweet); Verdelho (medium dry); Sercial (dry). Little mention was ever made of other varieties. I learnt that the production started by fermenting grape juice, then stopping the fermentation at a predetermined time, to leave a fortified wine with the required level of sweetness. The wines were then 'heated' – a process alien to all I'd previously read about winemaking. Finally the wine was matured in casks until ready to bottle.

As a regular visitor to the island, and to the wineries, I have met with owners, winemakers and other staff, many of whom I have come to know well. I always receive a warm welcome, have the opportunity to ask questions and taste some wonderful wines, often wines of considerable age. When I realised just how much more there was to producing Madeira than my early courses had taught me, I was determined to learn all I could about this unique wine. As an educator, I wanted to make sure I was giving accurate information to my students. My researches showed there were relatively few books about Madeira wine, so, in 2007, I decided I wanted to share my newly acquired knowledge more widely, by writing about it. I had read Alex Liddell's book, published in 1998 and felt the time was right to describe the industry 10 years on.

This book is intended for the person who is interested in finding out about the wonderful wines produced in Madeira, for those who already know and enjoy these wines but wish to learn more and for students preparing for wine examinations. Although the intention is that it should be read in its entirety, it is written so that the reader can just read selected chapters. This inevitably leads to repetition of some information.

As a chemistry teacher in a previous life, I know how many people become worried and tend to 'switch off' when they see chemical formulae and technical terms. I have tried to keep these to a minimum and hope that the many photographs throughout the book will make for a better understanding of how the wines are made and aged. These processes are described in the first five chapters.

In the next chapter, the reader will find advice and suggestions for storing and serving the wines. Whilst I believe strongly that selecting wines to pair with foods, or indeed drinking wines without food, is very much a matter of personal choice, I have included recommendations from the producers and also some menus showing possible pairings throughout a meal.

The tasting chapter deals with the difficult topic of describing and evaluating wines. As a wine educator I am aware of the way in which different people have different perceptions of the same wines. I have attempted to describe the characteristics of the wines which I hope will help readers who have never tasted them to gain an insight into what they can expect when they do have the chance to taste. Also, I trust it will help those who have tasted the wines before but are looking for ways of describing them. I have deliberately avoided giving a list of my own personal tasting notes, preferring to select notes written by producers and winemakers.

I have included a chapter giving a profile of each of the eight producers. It includes a little of the history and development of each company, together with an indication of their size, their location and how to contact them. In the appendices, readers can find a list of wines currently available. The lists are, of course, subject to change, especially as only small quantities of some wines are produced.

I make no apology for including a chapter that gives a great many statistics. I believe it helps, together with the other chapters, to give an overall picture of the wine industry. I have tried to highlight what I consider to be some very interesting facts. The Wine Institute is the governing body of the industry and the book would not be complete without a chapter describing the various checks and balances that are put in place with the aim of producing the best possible wines for the consumer.

During the past few years a small volume of unfortified wines, known as table wines, have been made. I believe a chapter about these wines merits inclusion, as their production may well become an important part of the island's wine industry in the future.

In the final chapter I have tried to look at some of the difficulties experienced by the industry and consider possible ways in which these may be overcome.

I could never have written this book without the help and support from a very large number of people. They have given generously of their time and knowledge, enduring my seemingly endless list of questions. During my many visits to the island, The Madeira Wine Institute (IVBAM) and the companies have facilitated my research by providing hospitality, arranging visits and giving me access to wineries, vineyards and detailed information.

I am extremely grateful to Paulo Rodrigues, previous President of The Madeira Wine Institute, Paula Cabaço, the current President and João Nunes, Vice President, who have provided an enormous amount of help and given me access to their departments and records.

I particularly wish to thank the following members of The Institute for their help: Isabel Delgado, Carlota Ferreira, Magalhães Ferreira, Eduardo Freitas, Rita Galvão, Rogério Gonçalves, João Pedro Machado, Luisa Machado, Nadia Meroni, Ângela Nascimento, Rosária Silva, Bárbara Spinola.

Help from the producers and from the University of Madeira has been invaluable. I wish to express my sincere thanks to: Artur de Barros e Sousa, Lda; HM Borges, Sucrs, Lda; J Faria & Filhos, Lda; Henriques & Henriques, Vinhos SA; Justino's Madeira Wines, SA; the Madeira Wine Company, SA; Pereira d'Oliveira (Vinhos), Lda; and Vinhos Barbeito (Madeira), Lda. In the list that follows, I hope I have remembered all who have helped me: Francisco Albuquerque, António Agrela, Sónia Amaral, Filipe Azevedo, Ivo Couto, Jackie Dias, Luis and Luisa Faria, Julio Fernandes, Helena Borges Fontes, Ricardo Diogo Freitas, Isabel Borges Gonçalves, Humberto Jardim, José Carlos Marques, Artur and Edmundo de Olim, Filipe and Luis d'Oliveira, Luis Pereira, Marianna Pinto, Ricardo Tavares, Juan Teixeira, Jacques Faro da Silva.

I am grateful to a number of people in the UK, who have given their support and help, in particular: Danny Cameron, David Evans, Ben Campbell-Johnston, Claire Collini (Sotheby's), Neil Courtier, Antonia Essex (Christies), David Evans, Antony Moss, Tim Stanley-Clarke, Geoffrey Cole and Hazel Tattersall.

My sincere thanks for the production of this book go to Lindsey Maguire for his help, advice and printing skills, Alistair Plumb for his design expertise and Ricky Foyle for photographic advice.

I wish to express special thanks to Keith Grainger, for his help and encouragement and for his painstaking efforts in reading the manuscript.

Finally, I would like to thank Tessa, my long-suffering wife, for her support and encouragement and, on many occasions, for 'coaxing' my computer to do what I required of it.

If, in the above lists, I have omitted anyone, I offer my sincere apologies.

I believe this book will prove a valuable addition to the limited number of wine books on the topic of Madeira. Whilst trying to maintain readability, I have included some technical information and statistics. Any errors are mine!

INTRODUCTION

Trevor Elliott

Trevor Elliott
SUMMER 2010

Chapter 1
A Short History of Madeira

The Island

It is not the intention of this book to give great detail about the history of the island and its wines. Liddell (*Madeira, Alex Liddell, Faber & Faber 1998*) has carefully researched and most comprehensively written about this. The following is a very brief summary of some of the more important dates and developments since the discovery of the island.

The Portuguese island of Madeira, situated in the Atlantic Ocean, approximately 970 kilometres southwest of Lisbon and 600 kilometres from the coast of North Africa, is part of the Archipelago of Madeira, which includes the islands of Porto Santo, the Desertas and the Selvegens. It is the largest and most important of the group and has an area of approximately 735 square kilometres, being 57 kilometres west to east and 23 kilometres north to south at the widest points.

The island was discovered in 1419 by João Gonçalves Zarco, Tristão Vaz Teixeira and Bartolomeu Perestrelo. Some years later, King João I of Portugal ordered the island to be divided up into areas or *captancies* for colonisation. The three areas were administered by Zarco, Teixeira and Perestrelo, who leased it to the early colonists for development. Over the following centuries, various systems of ownership and tenancies were developed.

Colonisation

The first colonisers were members of the Portuguese nobility who brought with them labourers and craftsmen from northern Portugal. Also attracted to the island were wealthy merchants from Europe who recognised the trading potential. Special concessions were given to the earlier settlers.

Large areas of dense forests and other vegetation were burned to produce space required for agriculture and increase the fertility of the soil. Terraces, supported by stone walls, were constructed to allow planting of vines on the steep slopes. An irrigation system of channels, called *levadas*, was built to collect water from the higher regions and transport it throughout the island, providing water for crops and drinking. This has been developed over the centuries and now extends for approximately 2,150 kilometres (1,344 miles), of which 40 kilometres (25 miles) are in tunnels.

Sugar cane became the main agricultural product and was exported to mainland Portugal, the Gulf of Guinea, and African, Mediterranean and Northern European markets. Other important crops were wheat and vines. As will be seen, the production of sugar declined and wine became very important.

LEFT The statue of João Gonçalves Zarco, Avenida Arriaga, Funchal.

OVERLEAF Cabo Girão cliffs and Praia Formosa.

JOÃO GONÇALVES ZARCO

The Wines

It would seem that the early colonisers brought vines from the north of Portugal. Records show that Malvasia Cândida was one of the first varieties to be planted. It is likely that the early settlers from northern Portugal would have brought other varieties. Some 25 years after the colonisation of the island, the first wines were exported.

Fifteenth century

During the 15th century, there was an increase in the planting of vines and the export of wines, although there are no records to show the quantities. The discovery of America by Christopher Columbus in 1492 was very important for future exports from the island.

Sixteenth century

During the 16th century, the island flourished, trade increased, and so did the population. In 1508, Funchal acquired the status of a city. From the early part of the century there was a decrease in the production and export of sugar. This was due to a number of reasons, including the cultivation problems of sugar cane and the availability of labour. By the end of the century, the industry was in crisis due to the availability of much cheaper sugar from Brazil. Sugar plantations were therefore converted into vineyards and wine became the main export.

There is much speculation about the style of wines and whether they were sweet or dry. It is known that they were not fortified.

Seventeenth century

Exports grew considerably throughout the 17th century. From the middle of the century the number of British merchants increased. They became influential as their colonial markets developed in America and they were given trading concessions. Great Britain became prominent in the trade that developed between Madeira, the New World and Europe. Madeira wine became widely known and enjoyed a prestigious reputation.

During the 17th century, some of the wines exported to the Indies, which were then returned to Europe, had experienced very high temperatures when passing through the tropics. They were found to have improved in quality during the journey. Following this discovery, wine was sent to the Indies

ABOVE Funchal Harbour in the early 20th century.

in the holds of ships and returned to Europe, deliberately to enhance the quality. These wines, called *Vinho da Roda* or 'Round Trip Wines' were much sought after and sold for very high prices.

Eighteenth century

In the 18th century, the main markets for Madeira wine continued to be the West Indies, North America and the East Indies. It was during this century that British merchants became very important on the island. Despite special tariff arrangements between Britain and Portugal – the Methuen Treaty of 1703 – it was not until later in the century that exports of wine to Britain increased. The increasing worldwide demand for the wines resulted in fraud,

with the consequent sale of adulterated wines or wines from other sources described as Madeira. Action was taken to regulate the wine trade.

This century saw two important developments in the techniques of wine making; fortification and the *Estufagem* process. Most companies were fortifying their wines by the middle of the century, but it was only towards the end of the century that *Estufas* were built.

Nineteenth century

The 19th century was a time of mixed fortunes for Madeira wines. Some poor harvests, continuing fraud, wars in Europe and the American Civil War all had a major affect on exports. The opening of the Suez Canal in 1869 meant that ships travelling west no longer called at Madeira. Around the middle of the century there was a welcome increase in the Russian market.

In the second half of the century the vineyards were devasted by powdery mildew (*Oidium tuckeri* aka *Erysiphe necator*) and Phylloxera (*Daktulosphaira vitifolia*).

The powdery mildew spread rapidly, and was found throughout the island by 1852. It damaged the vines and decreased the production of wine to almost zero. Clearly, this had a major effect on the island's economy. Fortunately during this period, exports from reserve stocks remained quite strong. However, many merchants still left the island.

It took some time for the industry to recover. Dead vines were replaced by varieties from mainland Portugal.

Phylloxera was found in Madeira in 1872, a decade or so after it had started devastating the vineyards of Europe. To overcome Phylloxera, vineyards were replanted with vines grafted onto American rootstocks or simply replanted with American vines. Varieties such as Jacquet and Cunningham were used.

Fortunately, by the end of the century production and sales of Madeira wine were showing signs of recovery.

Twentieth century

Many changes took place in the wine industry during the 20th century. Markets were affected by the two World Wars, the Russian Revolution (1917), Prohibition in America (1920 –1933), the Portuguese Revolution (1974) and by Portugal joining the European Union (EU) in 1986.

Markets changed throughout the century. Germany was an important market until the First World War, the British market declined, exports ceased to Russia from 1917, and to America between 1920 and 1934. Scandinavia became an important market after the First World War and the British and French markets remained steady.

After a slump in the early 1930s, markets started to recover, only to be affected by the Second World War. After the war, fashions in wines changed and fortified wines became less popular.

The 1940s, 50s, 60s and 70s showed fluctuations in the sale of Madeira wines. Scandinavia remained a very important market, together with France – especially for bulk sales – Germany and Britain. After a drop in exports in 1980, there was a levelling out and, by the end of the century, the important markets were France – especially for bulk wines – Germany, Britain, Scandinavia, Japan and America.

Following the Revolution (1974) and a return to democracy in Portugal, Madeira was granted political autonomy and became *Região Autonoma da Madeira* (The Autonomous Region of Madeira). Modernisation of the island meant that valuable lands used for vineyards were sold for building.

In order to become more efficient companies amalgamated. The Madeira Association was formed from three companies in 1913 and over the following decades other companies joined. Membership changed until in 1981 the Association became the Madeira Wine Company.

During the century, there were attempts to regulate the industry. A commission was formed in 1909 (*Comissão de Viticultura*) and after Salazar became Prime Minister of Portugal (1933), the *Junta Nacional da Vinho* was set up to control Portuguese wine production. In 1979 when the Junta was abolished, the Madeira Wine Institute became the controlling body for the island's wines. These various bodies were responsible for many changes throughout the industry.

When Portugal joined the EU in 1986, further regulations were introduced, which have led to an improvement in quality of the wines. The Madeira wine industry has benefited considerably from EU subsidies.

Twenty first century

Now, in the 21st century, there is an obvious commitment from the remaining producers to improve the quality of Madeira wines, to expand existing markets, to seek new markets

ABOVE Working at Barbeito's new modern winery.

and to enhance the reputation of Madeira wines throughout the world. Huge investments have been made in recent years and are still continuing in all aspects of the industry including the vineyards and the wineries. These developments will be described throughout the book.

The main export markets today (2010) are France, Germany, United Kingdom, Japan, USA, Belgium, Sweden and Switzerland.

The controlling body for the industry is now The Wine, Embroidery and Handicraft Institute of Madeira – *Instituto do Vinho do Bordado e do Artisanato da Madeira, IP* (IVBAM) which was formed in June 2006 by merging the Madeira Wine Institute and the Madeira Embroideries, Tapestries and Handicrafts Institutes.

Throughout the book, IVBAM will be referred to as The Institute.

THE WINES

Chapter 2
Viticulture

The Growers

There are approximately 1600 registered growers and for most of them, growing vines is not their main occupation. On average a grower owns 0.3 hectares (ha), which may be divided into more than one plot. With the exception of Henriques & Henriques, the producers do not own vineyards and purchase grapes from the growers.

Growers can apply for EU aid for producing grapes for the production of Madeira wine and unfortified table wines (DOP Madeirense, IGP Terras Madeirenses). The value of aid depends on the grape variety and is currently €500 per tonne (1000 kilograms) for Sercial, Verdelho, Boal, Malvasia Cândida, Malvasia Roxa, Terrantez, Bastardo and Listrão and €81 per tonne for other recommended and approved varieties.

Although there are longstanding agreements between the growers and the producers, they are not in the form of written contracts. This means producers are free to buy from any of the growers and the growers are free to sell to any of the producers. Some growers sell to more than one producer. Negotiations may be directly between growers and producers or via agents. For the 2009 harvest, 1304 growers sold 3,904,278 kilograms (kg) of grapes for the production of Madeira wine, an average of nearly 3000kg per grower. Approximately a third of the growers (433) supplied 1000kg or less, 14 growers sold less than 100kg each and the smallest amount sold by one grower was 24kg!

The only producer who owns vineyards is Henriques & Henriques with a ten hectare vineyard, Quinta Grande, which is mostly planted with Verdelho, some Sercial and a small amount of Terrantez. They also own a small vineyard of one hectare, planted with Tinta Negra. These vineyards only supply approximately 15% of the grapes the company requires. The rest are purchased from growers.

ABOVE Henriques and Henriques Quinta Grande vineyard.

GRAPES SOLD FOR MADEIRA WINE - 2009 HARVEST			
kg of grapes	Number of growers	kg of grapes	Number of growers
0 – 500	199	5000 – 6000	46
500 – 1000	234	6000 – 7000	38
1000 – 1500	183	7000 – 8000	36
1500 – 2000	121	8000 – 9000	24
2000 – 2500	100	9000 – 10,000	19
2500 – 3000	77	10,000 – 15,000	38
3000 – 3500	60	15,000 – 20,000	20
3500 – 4000	47	20,000 – 25,000	9
4000 – 4500	26	25,000 – 30,000	1
4500 – 5000	25	30,000 – 35,000	0
		35,000 – 40,000	1

TOTAL = 1304 growers

GRAPE SUPPLIES FOR 2009 HARVEST	
Producer	Number of growers
Vinhos Barbeito Madeira Lda (Barbeito)	106
H M Borges, Sucrs, Lda (Borges)	100
Pereira D'Oliveira (Vinhos), Lda (D'Oliveira)	80
Justino's, Madeira Wines, SA (Justino's)	725
Henriques & Henriques, Vinhos SA (Henriques & Henriques)	340
The Madeira Wine Company, SA (MWC)	448
Approximate numbers.	

Although the MWC purchases from approximately 600 growers each year, most of their grapes are supplied by approximately 40 of these. They have a special relationship with one grower who sells his whole crop – approximately 26,000kg – to the company. This is unusual, as the larger growers normally sell to more than one company.

The producers maintain regular contact with the growers throughout the year. All companies have agents: Barbeito (2), Borges (2), D'Oliveira (3), Henriques & Henriques (6), Justino's (9), MWC (3). The agents visit the growers on a regular basis representing the companies, offering help and advice and monitoring the crop. As the harvest approaches the visits become more frequent. From time to time, the winemakers also visit the growers.

OVERLEAF The vineyards at Estreito de Câmara de Lobos.

The Grapes

Currently (2010), there is a total of 493.7ha of *Vitis vinifera* vines planted for the production of fortified Madeira wines and table wines. Approximately 81% of plantings are in Câmara de Lobos, São Vincent and Santana. For the 2009 harvest, approximately 85% of the total production was used to produce fortified Madeira wine.

The maximum permitted yield is 80hL/ha with increases allowed in years of exceptional weather and production conditions. Increases must be approved by The Institute. For 2008 and 2009, the permitted yields were 150hL/ha.

Traditionally, a number of different grape varieties have been used for Madeira wines.

The soils

The soils are of volcanic origin, rich in organic matter and minerals such as magnesium. Some soils are too fertile for vines. Often there is there is a high iron content. Due to their volcanic origin, the soils often have a high acidity and there is a need to treat with lime to reduce this. When treating vines for diseases using copper sulphate

GRAPE GROWING AREAS 2010		
Concelho (Council)	Área (ha)	Main Varieties
Calheta	18.86	Boal, Verdelho
Câmara de Lobos	187.88	Tinta Negra, Sercial, Verdelho, Boal
Funchal	2.89	Complexa, Malvasias, Verdelho
Machico	9.82	Various red varieties
Ponta do Sol	0.79	Tinta Negra, Boal
Porto Moniz	35.75	Red varieties, Verdelo, Sercial
Porto Santo	11.76	Various white varieties
Ribeira Brava	11.35	Tinta Negra, Boal
Santa Cruz	1.96	Complexa, other red varieties
Santana	70.34	Malvasia, Complexa, white varieties
São Vicente	142.32	Tinta Negra, Verdelho, Complexa
Total	493.72	

Instituto do Vinho, do Bordado e do Artesanato da Madeira, IP

it is important not to use too much, because it will increase the acidity of the soil. If this happens, it prevents the vines from absorbing the main nutrients such as nitrogen, potassium and phosphorus.

The climate

The island has a temperate climate, with hot, humid summers and mild winters. Rainfall, of which 75% occurs mostly in the autumn and winter and 20% in the spring, varies from 3000mm

MAIN RECOMMENDED GRAPE VARIETIES	
White	Red
Sercial (Esgana Cão)	Tinta Negra
Verdelho	Bastardo
Bual (Malvasia Fina)	Malvasia Cândida Roxa
Malvasia Cândida	
Terrantez	
MAIN AUTHORISED GRAPE VARIETIES	
White	Red
Listrão	Complexa
Malvasia de São Jorge	

ABOVE Coast and vineyards near Seixal.

MAIN WHITE GRAPE VARIETIES

Malvasia

Malvasia Cândida (*Malmsey*) is believed to be the first variety bought to the island in the 15th century. It grows best in the south in Câmara de Lobos, Estreito da Calheta and Campanário, but is also grown at altitudes of 200 to 300 metres in the north in São Jorge, Arco de São Jorge and Santana. It is site-sensitive, and prone to mildew, growing best at altitudes of 100–200 metres and where it has plenty of sun, which protects it from disease. The grapes and bunches are medium to large, and golden in colour when ripe. The must normally has a potential alcohol of up to 13% abv.

Boal

Boal (*Bual*) is grown mainly in warm locations in the south of the island in Calheta, Estreito da Calheta, Arco da Calheta, Câmara de Lobos, Estreito de Câmara de Lobos and Campánario. A small amount is grown in the north. It is prone to mildews. The grapes and bunches are medium to large, and golden in colour when ripe. The must normally has a potential alcohol of 11–13% abv.

Verdelho

Verdelho is grown mainly in the north, in São Vicente, Seixal, Arco de São Jorge, Ponta Delgada and Ribeira da Janela, with smaller quantities in the south, in Prazeres, Fajã da Ovelha and Estreito de Câmara de Lobos. The grapes and bunches are small or medium. The must has a marked acidity, and normally a potential alcohol of 10–12%.

Sercial

Sercial is grown mostly in the north of the island in Seixal, Porto Moniz, Ponta, Delgada, São Vicente and Arco de São Jorge. In the south, it is mainly planted in Jardim da Serra at an altitude of 600–700 metres. The grapes and bunches are medium in size, have high levels of acidity and the must has a potential alcohol of 10–11% abv.

MAIN RED GRAPE VARIETY

Tinta Negra

Tinta Negra, as it now known (to prevent confusion with Tinta Negra Mole which is planted in the Algarve), is the most widely planted of the 5 varieties of grape used for Madeira. After phylloxera devastated the vineyards at the end of the nineteenth century, much Tinta Negra was planted. Now it is grown mainly in Estreito de Câmara de Lobos and Câmara de Lobos in the south and São Vicente in the north. It produces good yields and is resistant to disease. Bunches are medium to large, and the grapes are soft and red in colour when ripe. The juice (must) normally has a potential alcohol of 9–12% alcohol by volume (abv).

ABOVE Tinta Negra grapes grown on a low *Latada*.

at high altitudes to 500mm near sea level. The north of the island has more rainfall than the south. The annual mean temperature ranges from 9°C in the mountains to 17.5°C along the coast. There are many microclimates throughout the winegrowing areas, due to the variations in altitude, temperature, humidity and rainfall.

Methods of training

Much of the island has slopes of more than 25%. Vines and other crops are grown in areas with slopes of 16–25%. This is only possible by constructing terraces (*poios*), which are supported by stone walls.

The traditional method of training is the *Latada*, which is also known as the

pergola. The vines are grown horizontally along wires suspended on stakes, ideally at about two metres above the ground. However, some are lower and some very much higher. The vines are planted at a density of 2500–4000 per hectare. Weeding, pruning, clearing leaves and harvesting is very difficult, because the canopy is often close to the ground. In the north the pergolas have to be enclosed or have fences of heather or bracken, to protect the grapes from the wind and spray from the sea.

A second method, *Espaldeira* or *espalier*, where the vines are grown vertically in rows on wires, was introduced during the second half of the 20th century but this can only be done where the land is fairly flat. With this method, the density of planting is 4000–5000 vines per hectare.

When replanting or planting new vineyards, the preferred training method is *Espaldeira*, where it is easier to control the canopy growth and to carry out the various vineyard operations. However, if, because of the terrain, it is necessary to plant in *Latadas*, the preferred height is just below two metres, for ease of working.

Vine treatments

Downy Mildew (*Plasmopara viticola*) is a problem because of the warm humid summers. It attacks all the green parts of vines, especially the young leaves. Loss of leaves will affect photosynthesis and therefore the ripening of the grapes and the sugar levels. It can also affect growth in the following year. It is seen as 'oil spots' on the top surface of the leaves and a white cottony growth on the underside. Protective sprays, usually copper based, are used, but they are only effective for about ten days. Six to eight treatments are normally required. Curative fungicides became available in the 1990s, but they are more expensive.

Powdery Mildew (*Oidium tuckerii*), also known on the island as *Mangra*, is another problem. It attacks all green parts of the vine and is seen as a cobweb-like growth, which spreads in warm weather, and although little affected by humidity, it develops where vine canopies are dense and shaded. After a week or two, it develops as ash-like spores on upright shoots and is spread by the wind. It can affect fruit set and reduce yields. It can be treated with sulphur, in the form of wettable

ABOVE Tinta Negra grapes affected by Botrytis.

throughout the whole bunch, particularly when the berries are in close contact. Treatment is spraying with fungicides, starting at flowering and finishing three to four weeks before harvest.

It should be mentioned, that if Botrytis affects ripe healthy white grapes, it could develop into the form called *noble rot* which in some regions of the world allows producers to make sweet wines of high quality.

In the case of downy mildew, powdery mildew and botrytis, treatments are preventative.

sulphur or organic fungicides and usually requires six to eight treatments.

Grey Rot (*Botrytis cinerea*) is a problem for vines in damp climates. The spores germinate on wet surfaces or when humidity is high, and can attack almost ripe or damaged grapes, reducing the yield and affecting the quality. The mould can spread

Escoriose (*Phomopsis viticola*) develops in warm humid and wet conditions. It attacks the stems of the vines and can cause considerable loss of yield. It is treated with fungicide sprays as a curative treatment. Systemic treatments can also be used, but these are much more expensive.

The Harvest

There is an 'official' date, decided by The Institute in consultation with the companies and the growers. It is usually the last week of August or the first week of September. The first day is a Monday, which in 2009 was 31st August. If grapes are considered to be ripe before this date, a company can contact The Institute to obtain permission to pick earlier, in order to obtain the grapes in the best possible condition. Justino's did in fact receive grapes on 26th August 2009. Normally the harvest will begin up to two weeks later on the north facing slopes, because they are cooler and wetter.

At harvest time, many family members and neighbours are often involved in picking the grapes. Some, who live in other European countries, return to the island each year in September for the harvest.

Harvesting is extremely hard work, and especially difficult when picking the grapes from underneath some of the *Latadas*. Ideally, the grapes will be approximately at head height, but they may be lower, making it necessary for pickers to bend to prevent them hitting their heads. Some *Latadas* are so high that pickers require ladders.

After picking, the grapes are then carried in boxes to the nearest road, to be put on vehicles for transporting to the wineries. Vineyard slopes are often very steep, and the pathways to them narrow and extremely difficult

RIGHT Picking Tinta Negra from 2m high (approx) *Latadas*.

AVERAGE POTENTIAL ALCOHOL (% ABV)					
Year	Tinta Negra + others	Malvasia	Boal	Verdelho	Sercial
2008	9.75%	10.25%	9.80%	11.00%	9.68%
2009	9.47%	9.81%	9.67%	10.61%	9.15%

AVERAGE PRICE (EUROS PER KG)					
Year	Tinta Negra + others	Malvasia	Boal	Verdelho	Sercial
2008	1.06 €/kg	1.18 €/kg	1.11 €/kg	1.27 €/kg	1.10 €/kg
2009	0.98 €/kg	1.12 €/kg	1.08 €/kg	1.26 €/kg	1.16 €/kg
Further statistics can be found at the end of the book.					

ABOVE Using a ladder to pick Tinta Negra from high *Latadas*.

to walk. Most people would not wish to carry 50–60kg boxes of grapes, one at a time, taking 10–15 minutes, from the vineyard to a lorry!

Picking grapes trained by the *Espaldeira* method is somewhat easier, but nevertheless very hard work.

To be accepted for making Madeira wine, the grapes must have a minimum potential alcohol of 9% abv. The price which growers are paid depends on the condition of the grapes, the variety, the level of potential alcohol and market forces.

ABOVE Carrying grapes from vineyard to road, for transporting to winery.

ABOVE Picking from *Espaldeira* trained vines.

Chapter 3
Vinification

Receiving the Grapes

Transporting the grapes to the wineries depends on arrangements between the growers and the producers. The producer pays the delivery costs. Sometimes the growers deliver, sometimes agents will deliver or organise transport and sometimes the producer will collect.

The grapes are delivered in small plastic boxes – each company has different coloured boxes – which hold approximately 50kg. Using boxes of this size reduces the risk of damage to the grapes. When the existing boxes need replacing, Justino's intend to use boxes holding 25kg. Every effort is made to deliver the grapes as quickly as possible after picking, to minimise oxidation. Very occasionally, it may be necessary to add potassium metabisulphite powder to the grapes before they reach the winery, to prevent oxidation and fermentation.

ABOVE Sampling grape juice to measure the potential alcohol.

Scheduling the deliveries

The producers arrange a schedule of deliveries with the agents or growers, depending on their ability to process the grapes. Most try to avoid receiving grapes at weekends, but this is not always possible. Justino's process large quantities of grapes, for Madeira wines and table wines, which involves working on Saturdays and sometimes Sundays. Schedules may include not receiving grapes early on Monday mornings (Barbeito), as they would have to be picked the afternoon before. Some companies stop receiving grapes early in the evening, so they can be processed and the equipment cleaned and made ready for the following day.

The MWC schedule has a lunchtime break when grapes are not processed. The latest time for receiving grapes is normally late afternoon. Keeping to the schedules depends on the availability of pickers. If some arrive late at the vineyards or do not arrive at all, the delivery of grapes to the winery is delayed, resulting in working later than scheduled.

The Winemaking process

The chart shows the production process from harvesting to fortification. It should be noted that red, but not white grapes, are fermented with the skins.

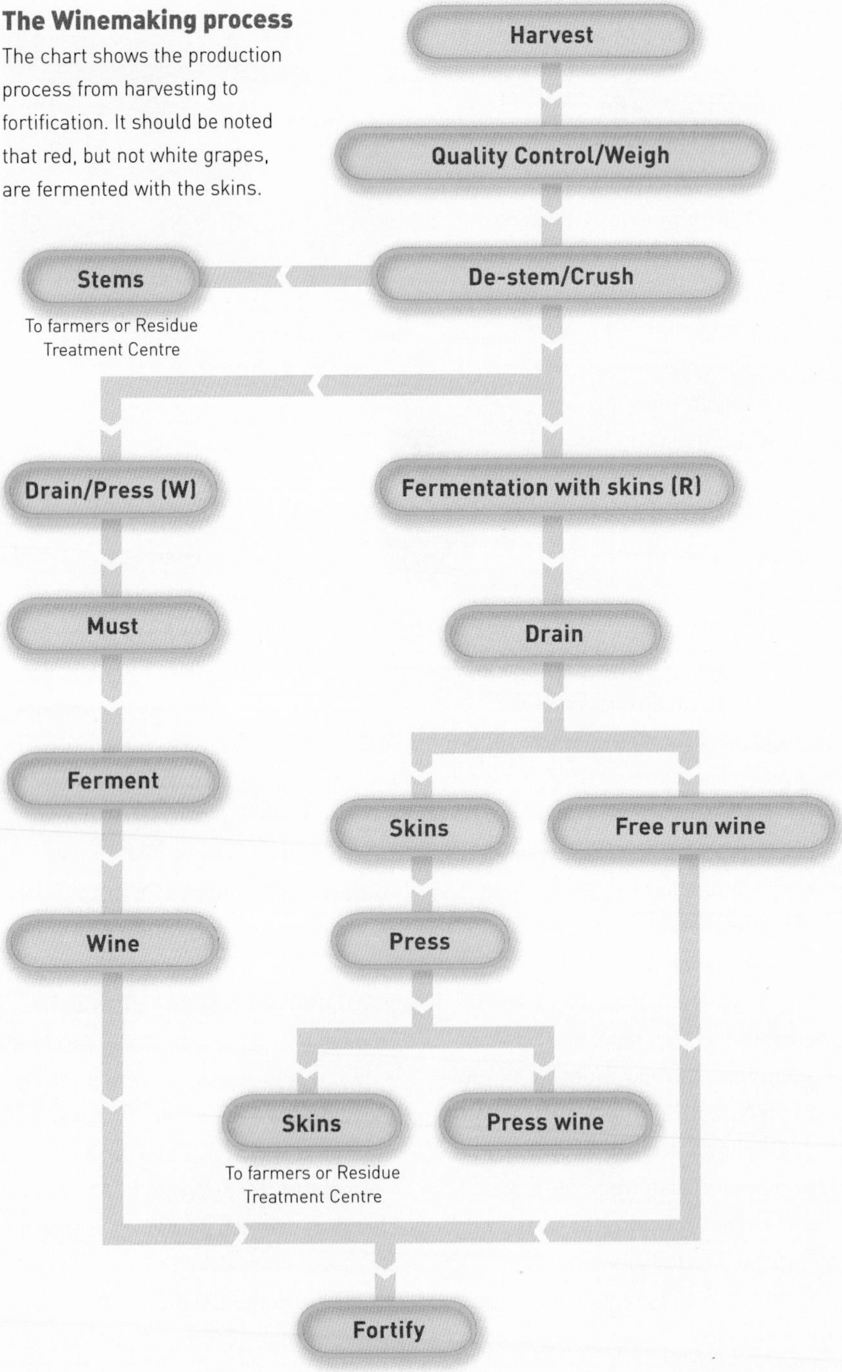

Harvest

↓

Quality Control/Weigh

↓

Stems

To farmers or Residue Treatment Centre

De-stem/Crush

↓

Drain/Press (W)

Fermentation with skins (R)

↓

Must

Drain

↓

Ferment

Skins   **Free run wine**

↓

Wine

Press

↓

Skins   **Press wine**

To farmers or Residue Treatment Centre

↓

Fortify

Despite having a large reception centre at their winery, Justino's also has a reception area for grapes in São Vincente. The boxes of grapes are taken to the centre; checked, weighed and then the grapes are transferred to large stainless steel containers, holding 1200kg, for transporting to the winery.

Most companies only process red or white grapes on any one day and usually only one white variety each day, but MWC has the equipment to process both red and white grapes at the same time.

ABOVE Using a refractometer to measure density and potential alcohol.

LEFT A digital refractometer.

Arrival of grapes

When the grapes arrive, they are inspected for quality and checked for mildew, dirt and other defects. Samples of juice are taken, either by mechanical means, or more often by simply selecting grapes from the boxes by hand and squashing them.

The potential alcohol is determined by measuring the sugar content using a refractometer. In order to be used for Madeira wine, the grapes must contain a minimum potential alcohol of 9% abv.

In 2009, some grapes were rejected because they failed to reach the minimum abv required. The crates were loaded back onto the lorry to be returned to the grower!

If accepted, the grapes are weighed and processed.

Whenever grapes are received, two representatives of The Institute must be present to check the weighing and measurement of potential alcohol. At the larger producers, where deliveries are fairly regular throughout the day, the representatives will be present on a regular daily basis. The smaller producers will contact The Institute to inform them of expected delivery times. Producers cannot start checking the grapes until the representatives arrive.

For the 2008 harvest, a new checking system was introduced. Growers were issued with a *Caderno de Vindima*, a white card which must be produced when grapes are delivered to the winery. This gives personal details of the grower, the size of vineyard plot(s), the grape varieties and the weight of grapes that can be produced. For each delivery, a

section of the card will be completed giving details of the grapes received by the company.

The grower will also be given a receipt from the producer, for the quantity of grapes sold, which shows the price per kilogramme to be paid.

The process of receiving the grapes is very time consuming and differs slightly between the producers. At Barbeito, when each box is weighed, a receipt is issued from a machine, rather like a receipt from a supermarket checkout. The total from all the receipts for a particular grower can then be automatically calculated and the figures entered on the official card. In future it is hoped this will be fully computerised.

Processing the Grapes

Before fermentation, various processes and treatments are undertaken. These include de-stemming, crushing, pressing in the case of white grapes and adjustments to the must.

De-stemming

All companies de-stem the grapes, to avoid the bitter flavours from the stems tainting the wine. Barbeito only started de-stemming during the 2007 harvest. The stems are then used for producing fertilisers.

Crushing

After de-stemming, the grapes will be crushed between rollers. This splits the berries and releases the juice. It must be carried out carefully to avoid crushing the skins and pips.

ABOVE Pneumatic press to extract juice..

Pressing

When using white grapes, the next stage is to release the remaining juice from the skins. Again it is important to regulate the pressure. The higher the pressure, the more juice will be obtained, but with very high pressure the skin cells are broken down to release unwanted bitter compounds.

When using red grapes, the pressing normally takes place after the fermentation. By keeping the skins with the juice during fermentation, there will be maximum extraction of colour.

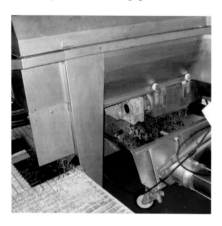

LEFT De-stemmer crusher showing stems (*on the left*) and must (*on the right*).

There are several different types of press. They normally consist of a slatted horizontal cylinder into which the grapes are loaded. One common type is the pneumatic press. This consists of a slatted cylinder containing a membrane or bag that can be inflated with compressed air. The press is filled with grapes and the bag inflated. The grapes are pressed against the inside surface of the

cylinder, releasing juice, which flows out through the slats and is pumped to the fermentation vessel.

Another type of press, the horizontal screw press, also consists of a slatted cylinder but in this case, two pistons that move towards each other press the grapes.

Treatments

The use of pectolytic enzymes and sulphur dioxide (SO_2) varies between producers. The sulphur dioxide is usually added in the form of a 5% aqueous solution of potassium metabisulphite ($K_2S_2O_5$) and stuns unwanted yeasts and bacteria and prevents oxidation.

Justino's de-stem the grapes, then, before crushing, adds pectolytic enzymes (2–4gm/100kg), in aqueous solution. This helps to extract the colour from red grapes and the

Before de-stemming and crushing, the MWC adds pectolytic enzymes equivalent to 0.5gms per 140 gm of grapes, to help extract the maximum of aromatic compounds during maceration and increase the rate of clarification of juice. After de-stemming, sulphur dioxide is added (50mg/litre). The level of free SO_2 is checked and if necessary adjusted to 50mg/litre.

Barbeito adds pectolyic enzymes (3gms/hL) in aqueous solution after crushing. It is added to the fermentation tanks when they are half full, to aid mixing. The must will have started to ferment and this aids the work of the enzymes. The enzymes are used to help bring out the natural aromas and flavours and to help compact the lees after fortification. After crushing, potassium metabisulphite is added (12gm/hL).

Borges does not use pectolytic enzymes. Sulphur dioxide (50mg/litre) is added to the must before fermentation.

Henriques & Henriques does not use pectolytic enzymes. Sulphur dioxide is added (25gm/hL), in solid form, after de-stemming and crushing.

D'Oliveira adds pectolytic enzymes (3.0gm/hL) to help clarify the must. Sulphur dioxide is added (50mg/litre) to the must before fermentation.

clarification of the must of white grapes. It also helps during pressing, by reducing the pressure required, and facilitates filtration at later stages. After crushing, sulphur dioxide is added. The amount used depends on the sanitary condition of the grapes.

Fermentation

Fermentation is the process in which yeasts convert sugars into alcohols. It is carried out in stainless steel tanks of various sizes. There are variations in the way the producers carry out the fermentation process.

Skin contact

Justino's use skin contact when making sweet, medium sweet and Colheita wines from Tinta Negra. During fermentation, the skins will rise to the top of the fermentation tank. To give the maximum extraction of colour and flavour from the skins, the fermenting wines are pumped from the bottom to the top of the tank. This process, called pumping-over, is carried out at least

ABOVE Stainless steel Autovinification tanks at MWC.

RIGHT Stainless steel vinification tanks at Barbeito.

four times per day, for 10–15 minutes. At the present time, Justino's does not use skin contact when making wines from white grapes, but this is under consideration for the future.

The MWC vinifies dry and medium dry wines from Tinta Negra without skin contact, but for sweet and medium sweet wines, skin contact and autovinification are used to extract the maximum colour. Autovinifcation is another form of pumping-over. The pressure in the fermentation tank pushes the juice to the top where, using a system of valves, it is allowed to flow back down through the skins. For all white varieties, skin contact pre fermentation takes

place, to obtain the maximum dry extract from the grapes. The mixture of skins and juice is cooled down to avoid bitter flavours dissolving in the juice and then left to stand for several hours. The temperature is raised to 20°C to start the fermentation. Pressing takes place before fermentation for Sercial, Verdelho, and Boal. The MWC is the only producer to ferment Malvasia grapes on the skins, because the winemaker believes this gives better extraction.

Borges only use skin contact when making sweet and medium sweet wines from Tinta Negra and other red grapes.

Henriques & Henriques ferment on the skins for red grapes and pump-over every hour.

ABOVE Tinta Negra grapes being 'trodden' in robotic *Lagar*.

D'Oliveira only use skin contact when making sweet and medium sweet wines from red grapes.

Barbeito has recently purchased a stainless steel robotic *Lagar*. Grapes were traditionally crushed by foot in *Lagares*, three foot-high stone tanks, measuring 10 to 15 square metres. After treading for up to four hours, the grapes were left in the *Lagares* to ferment. This traditional method is still used in the Duoro for the production of small amounts of Port.

The robotic *Lagar*, with a capacity of 7000kg of grapes, is made of stainless

ABOVE Robotic *Lagar* at Barbeito's winery.

steel and has 'mechanical feet' which move up and down to 'tread' the grapes. It 'treads' for ten minutes every two hours. In 2008, Barbeito fermented approximately 14% (35,000kg) of Tinta Negra grapes in the *Lagar*.

Ricardo de Freitas says that although using the *Lagar* is expensive, it has the advantages of producing more full-bodied wines, that are "much darker in colour, due to the skin contact and have more intense and natural aromas".

Fermentation

Calculations show that 17gms/L of sugar in the must produces 1% of alcohol by volume (abv). Thus, if the grapes are picked at, say 10% abv, the must will contain 170gm/L of sugar.

The sugar content is important to the winemaker in terms of the style of wine to be made. There will need to be sufficient residual sugar in the wine when it is fortified. The alcohol in the finished Madeira wine will come mainly from fortification, not from the fermentation process.

Yeasts

All producers rely on natural yeasts, which are found on the grapes and in the wineries. When sulphur dioxide is added, it inhibits bacteria and the yeasts will start the fermentation process. As alcohol is produced, some of the yeasts die and the more powerful ones, strains of *Saccharomyces cerevisiae,* continue the process.

FERMENTATION CALCULATION

Alcoholic fermentation may be represented by the following equations:

Yeasts + sugars $\rightarrow$ alcohols + carbon dioxide gas

$$C_6H_{12}O_6* = 2C_2H_5OH** + 2CO_2$$

glucose   ethanol   carbon dioxide

*In the equation sugars are represented by glucose, but it must be understood that grape sugars contain roughly equal quantities of glucose and fructose. Both have the same chemical formula.

** Whilst ethanol (ethyl alcohol) is the main alcohol formed during fermentation, there are small quantities of other alcohols.

FERMENTATION TEMPERATURES IN °C

Company	Red Grapes	White Grapes
Barbeito	20.0–28.5	19–28.5
Borges	25.0–26.0	25.0–26.0
D'Oliveira	20.0–24.0	20.0–24.0
Justino's	28.0–32.0	16.0–20.0
Henriques & Henriques	30.0	25.0 max
MWC	24.0–25.0	20.0–21.0

Checking the progress of fermentation

All producers ferment in stainless steel in tanks ranging from 2000–55,000 litres. It is important to check the progress of the fermentation regularly and, if necessary, control the temperature. The temperature and density are checked and recorded. The density is measured using a hydrometer. This is a kind of glass 'float' with stem containing a graduated scale.

LEFT Using a hydrometer to measure density of wine.

As sugar is converted into alcohol, the density decreases and the hydrometer sinks more. This gives the winemaker a measure of the amount of sugar left in the fermenting must.

The regularity of the checks varies between the producers from twice a day (Borges, Justino's), twice to four times a day (Barbeito), "several times a day" (Henriques & Henriques) and "every two hours" (MWC). Checks are made more frequently if the fermentation is proceeding quickly and also when nearing the time for fortification.

Chapter 4
Fortification
and Aging

Fortification

Depending on the style of wine to be made, the winemaker will decide the stage at which to halt the fermentation by the addition of alcohol in the form of 96% grape spirit. The producer is free to purchase the grape spirit from any supplier, normally from Portugal, Spain or France. The Institute must be notified when the alcohol is purchased, and, after taking a sample to check the quality, will give permission for it to be used for fortification.

The sweet and medium sweet Madeira wines are fortified first, in order to preserve a high level of residual sugar. Depending on the speed of fermentation, fortification is usually within a maximum of five days and normally one to three days from the start. Fermentation of dry or medium dry Madeira wines is allowed to continue until more of the sugars have been converted into alcohol. This can take up to seven or eight days, although often only three or four days, to reach the required level of residual sugar.

Each producer will decide on the residual sugar required for each of his or her styles of wine.

When the decision is made, the volume of alcohol required is calculated and the wine and alcohol are mixed. The approximate amounts of alcohol added are: Sweet (18–20%); Medium Sweet (14–16%); Medium Dry (10–13%); Dry (8–11%).

To ensure the fortified wine retains the required amount of residual sugar, it is important to stop the fermentation quickly. However,

RESIDUAL SUGAR IN GM/ LITRE				
Producer	Sercial or Dry	Verdelho or Medium Dry	Bual or Medium Sweet	Malmsey or Sweet
Borges	45.0–55.0	65.0–75.0	85.0–95.0	105.0–115.0
Barbeito	34.2–61.3	61.3–81.1	81.1–99.8	99.8–105.0
D'Oliveira	43 .0	74.0	94.0	118.0
Justino's	≤60.0	60.0–80.0	80.0–96.0	≥96.0
Henriques & Henriques	25.0–49.2	78.0	90.0	108.5
MWC	30.0–45.0	60.0–80.0	80.0–100.0	110+ Average 140

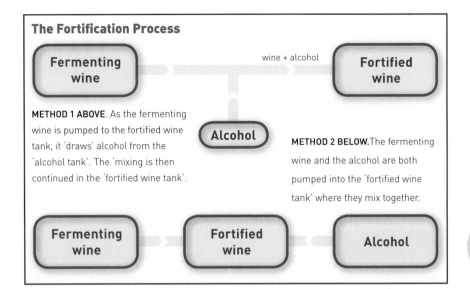

The Fortification Process

Fermenting wine

wine + alcohol

Fortified wine

Alcohol

METHOD 1 ABOVE. As the fermenting wine is pumped to the fortified wine tank, it 'draws' alcohol from the 'alcohol tank'. The 'mixing is then continued in the 'fortified wine tank'.

METHOD 2 BELOW. The fermenting wine and the alcohol are both pumped into the 'fortified wine tank' where they mix together.

Fermenting wine

Fortified wine

Alcohol

the mixing process creates a vigorous reaction and care must be taken to ensure the wine does not spill from the tank.

Mixing

Mixing is carried out in different ways, normally adding the alcohol to fermenting wine.

At the MWC mixing is achieved in two different ways. The wine is pumped from the fermenter through one of two connected pipes. As it moves along the pipe it draws alcohol from the second pipe, which is connected to a tank of alcohol.

Alternatively, the wine may be pumped into a tank and the alcohol added. The alcohol will be pumped into the bottom of the tank to help mixing.

Most producers pump the alcohol directly into the bottom of the fermentation tanks. Although this aids mixing, some producers will also pump-over to mix.

If the tanks are required for other fermentations, they will pump the fermenting wine into another tank and add the alcohol.

Barbeito pumps alcohol on to the top of the fermenting wine to form a layer, and then pumps the remainder of the alcohol into the bottom of the fermenter.

After fortification, the wines will normally contain between 17% and 18% abv. If the alcohol level is below 17% abv, it will be adjusted by the addition of more alcohol. The colour intensity might also be increased by the addition of a darker wine, probably a press wine.

Clarification

Before aging, the fortified wine is clarified (fined) to remove unwanted particles. A number of fining agents can be used. They are added to the wine and combine with the unwanted particles, to form a precipitate, which settles out over a number of hours. The precipitate can then be removed.

The most commonly used fining agent is Bentonite. It is a form of clay, mined in various parts of the United States.

It is often preferred to other agents such as Gelatine, an animal product, or Albumen, which is sourced from

Kieselguhr filtration

The rotary vacuum filter consists of a horizontal rotating cylinder, which is made from a fine stainless steel mesh. The lower part of the cylinder is immersed in a bath of the cloudy wine and Kieselguhr. The interior of the cylinder is connected to a powerful vacuum pump. The vacuum draws the wine through the mesh into the cylinder. The Kieselguhr particles are too large to go through the mesh and a layer is formed on the outside of the rotating drum. When the layer is several centimetres thick, the smaller particles in the cloudy wine will be trapped in the Kieselguhr and the clear wine will be drawn into the cylinder and pumped into tanks.

Until the layer of Kieselguhr has built up, the wine drawn through to the centre of the cylinder remains cloudy and will need to be recycled.

To prevent the layer of Kieselguhr on the outside of the cylinder becoming too thick, a blade shaves off the top enabling a continuous process.

Layer of Kieselguhr building up, ready to filter the cloudy wine.

Blades removing Kieselguhr, to prevent excessive build up.

egg whites. Sometimes Bentonite and Gelatine are used together.

After Bentonite fining, the wine may then be filtered using a Kieselguhr filter. Kieselguhr, mined in Germany, is an earth formed from the skeletons of tiny sea creatures called diatoms, that lived in the North Sea millions of years ago.

LEFT Vertical Kieselguhr filter.

Types of Kieselguhr filters

There are two main types of Kieselguhr filters: the rotary vacuum and the vertical filter. The action of the rotary vacuum filter is described above.

The second type of Kieselguhr vertical filter (*pictured left*), operates in the same way as the vacuum filter. It consists of a stainless steel tank which houses rotating hollow discs made of stainless steel mesh.

Aging

After fortification and clarification, the wines will be separated into different batches (*lotes*) to undergo the first stage of aging. There are two ways in which this is carried out. Both processes – *Estufagem* and *Canteiro* – involve heating and reaction with oxygen from the air (oxidation) and give the wines their unique aromas and flavours. The winemaker will decide which process to use. Wines that are sold at three or five years of age and are usually made from Tinta Negra, will normally be aged by the *Estufagem* process.

Estufagem

In this process, which dates back to the 18th century, the wines are pumped into containers, usually made of stainless steel – MWC *Estufas* are made of epoxy resin-lined concrete – which are heated by 'jackets' or stainless steel coils containing hot water. This enables the wine to be heated and kept at the required temperature of 45°C–50°C

for a period of three months. The temperature is normally controlled by computer.

Estufas can be large, ranging from 20,000–100,000 litres. Each *Estufa* can be used to age various quantities of wine. They are sealed and never filled to full capacity, to aid oxidation and to ensure there is room for the wine to expand when heated. It is important to keep all the wine at the required temperature. This is achieved in a number of ways. Some *Estufas* have

ABOVE Paddle fitted to *Estufa*, to aid mixing.

RIGHT Official seals on concrete *Estufa*.

ABOVE Large stainless steel *Estufas*, with heated water jackets.

RIGHT Official seal on tap of stainless steel *Estufa*.

coils inside and some have external jackets that cover 50–60% of the tanks. The jackets are placed at various levels around the outside. Convection currents will mix and circulate the wine. In addition to the jackets, Justino's pump-over the wines whilst in the *Estufas*, to aid the oxidation process and Henriques & Henriques have *Estufas* fitted with paddles.

The Institute controls the process, sealing the *Estufas* at the beginning and removing the seals, when requested, after a minimum of three months. Samples are taken before and after the process. After the seal is removed, the wines will be allowed to cool. This can take three to four weeks.

The wines will then be clarified using Bentonite or Bentonite and Gelatine, filtered using a Kieselguhr filter and left to rest for between six months and a year.

Wines may not be bottled and sold before 31st October of the second year following the harvest.

Canteiro

In this process the wines are aged in oak casks. The name comes from the wooden support beams, called *Canteiros*, that are used to support the casks.

The casks are of varying sizes, normally 300, 350, 500 and 650 litres, although they may be as large as 2500 litres.

In the *Canteiro* process, the wines are heated by keeping the casks in lofts and lodges that are heated by the sun. In the MWC some of the casks are in lofts above

the *Estufas*. Justino's are considering installing solar panels to increase lodge temperatures. If possible, the casks are placed on the top floor of high-level lofts where the temperature is higher. They will remain there for a period of two years. Temperatures can range (in °C) from the high 20s to the high 30s.

The humidity in the lofts can be quite high, usually 70–90%. During the process, there will be evaporation from the

Changes during aging

During aging, there will be oxidation, caramelisation of sugars, stabilisation of tartrates and evolution of acids, secondary alcohols, and polyphenols. Sotolon, a substance with the rather complicated formula 3-hydroxy-4, 5-dimethyl-2(5H)-furanone, is formed and gives rise to the typical and characteristic aromas of Madeira wines (*see* Chapter 7). The colour of the wines darkens to pale amber or brown; the sweeter the wine the darker the colour. The wines lose their primary fruit aromas and oxidative aromas and flavours develop. These include dried fruits, caramel, spices and chocolate.

casks. This will vary depending on temperature, humidity, the size of the cask and where the individual casks are placed in the lofts. Most producers say they lose 4–5% per year, although the loss can be as high as 6–7%.

The *Canteiro* process is used for all wines made from the white grape varieties – Malvasia, Boal, Verdelho, Sercial, and some high quality wines made from Tinta Negra.

Canteiro wines may not be sold until at least three years from 1st January of the year following the harvest.

61

AGING

BELOW Casks on *Canteiro* maturing in the loft at Barros e Sousa.

ABOVE Henriques & Henriques wine maturing at their centre in Câmara de Lobos.

BELOW Wine maturing at Barbeito's new winery.

Further aging

The winemaker will carefully test and taste each wine to determine its quality and potential for further aging. Partially due to the oxidation it undergoes during the time it spends in the wood, a wine will develop complex and intense flavours. Casks will range from 350 to 2800 litres and vats can hold up to 30,000 litres. The length of time a wine is left to age is a decision based on quality and the style of wine required, which in turn will be influenced by the market.

The evolution and quality of the wine is constantly monitored. This is very time consuming, especially for the larger producers. The MWC currently has approximately 1750 casks and 375

POSEIMA

Producers can apply to The Institute for an EU POSEIMA grant, if they age wines in cask for five consecutive years. At the time of writing, the grant is €0.05 per hectolitre per day of aging (€91.25 per 500 litre cask per year.)

The Institute will seal the cask at the beginning of the period and remove the seal after five years. A certificate will be attached to the cask.

During the five-year period, The Institute may carry out random checks on the integrity of the seal. The producer may, with permission, check the wine and carry out any necessary corrections to preserve the quality of the wine. A member of The Institute will remove the seal, monitor the corrections being carried out and reseal the cask.

After five years, the wine will be checked and any necessary adjustments made. If the winemaker decides it can benefit from further aging, the POSEIMA process can be repeated for a further five years.

Official certificate on cask, showing details of wine and date of POSEIMA.

Official seal on bung of cask during POSEIMA.

oak vats. Each is regularly monitored and subject to detailed annual checks in November. A computerised record is kept.

When casks are checked, the winemaker may decide corrections/adjustments are necessary.

This could involve adjustments to the alcohol level (abv) and the sweetness and also the removal of unwanted flavours. If the alcohol level is too high, the wine could be blended with a wine from the same vintage and grape variety but with lower alcohol. To increase the sweetness, up to 0.5% of rectified concentrated must can be added. This must be tested and approved by The Institute. If unwanted flavours are found they can be removed using a carbon filter.

Chapter 5
Blending
and Bottling

Blending

Blending is both an art and a science but it is the key to producing individual and consistent styles of wine. The blending team is all important. Blends will be submitted to The Institute to be tested to obtain the necessary seal of approval – *selo de garantia*.

In order to qualify for the seal, the wine will need to meet strict analysis standards laid down by The Institute. There may also be additional requirements by the customer. Details of the various Institute requirements are discussed later in 'Wine Styles'.

Blending is the most important part of making Madeira wines and the blender may wish to make more of one of the company's existing 'standard' blends or create a new blend.

Each company will keep a stock book, often now computerised, listing every cask of their wines. The winemaker will taste each wine on a regular basis and make notes about it. It is at this time, that a particular cask or casks might lead the blender to think of an idea for a new blend or to decide to bottle a single cask.

The blender will be aware, in the case of standard blends, which wines were blended to make them in previous years.

Sampling

From all the information available to the blender, small samples of the wines to be used will be withdrawn from the casks and blended until the 'standard' blend has been achieved. Others from the company may also taste the sample blend – the MWC has a panel of five. The sample will then be analysed and if it meets the necessary standards, the required quantity will be blended. This is known as the base wine.

A sample of the base wine will be analysed and tasted and the blender may decide to make some adjustments. These could be to the colour, sweetness/dryness, alcohol, or complexity. When this has been done to the blender's satisfaction, the company's panel will taste the wine. If approved, the adjustments will be made to all of the base wine. Once blended, the wine will be left for up to 6 months before fining and/or filtering and cold stabilisation as required before bottling.

Cold stabilisation is normally carried out for young wines (3 and 5 years old),

ABOVE Cold stabilisation equipment to remove tartrates.

RIGHT Plate filter. Filter sheets will be placed between plates.

to remove tartrates, which otherwise might, especially if wines are cooled, form a deposit after bottling. The tartrates can be removed in two ways. The wine is cooled to minus 8°C and stored in tanks for approximately a week and then filtered to remove precipitated tartrates. Alternatively, the wine can be cooled to 0°C and finely ground potassium bitartrate crystals added, stirring vigorously. The tartrates in the wine 'grow' onto the added bitartrate crystals and all the crystals are removed by filtration. The most modern process is the 'continuous' process, in which tartrate crystals are packed into the base of a tank and cooled wine is pumped up through. The stabilised wine is pumped from the top of the tank.

Young wines may also be filtered prior to bottling, to remove any unwanted particles.

A plate filter, also known as a sheet or pad filter will be used. It is possible to remove extremely small particles, even micro organisms with this type of filter.

Age of blends

If there is a statement of age on the label, such as 5-years-old, 10-years-old, 15-years-old, this is the average age of the blend, which will be made from wines of various ages. Francisco Albuquerque, winemaker at MWC, always prefers to make a blend from several different wines rather than just a few, because this adds to the complexity of the final blend.

As mentioned, tasting particular casks might lead to the idea of making a new blend. Alternatively, there might be a request for the creation of a new blend.

Recently, 3000 bottles of 'Centennial Blend' were produced by the MWC, which contained wines from each of the decades of the 20th century.

HM Borges made a blend to celebrate 500 years history of the city of Funchal. This wine is a blend of 40 years or over, made from their oldest Malvasia wines.

When ready for bottling, the producer will contact The Institute. They will collect samples of each blend and arrange for them to be analysed and tasted by members of an official tasting panel. It is most important that the company is as sure as possible, from its own analysis and tasting,

RIGHT Producing a blend. Checking the aromas (*top*), and the colour (*bottom*).

TYPICAL 5 YEAR OLD BLENDS		
A five-year-old blend (I)		
Age of component	% of each component	Proportion of final blend
3	10	0.3
5	75	3.75
10	15	1.5
Average		**5.55**
A five-year-old blend (II)		
Age of component	% of each component	Proportion of final blend
3	8	0.24
5	80	4.00
10	10	1.00
15	2	0.30
Average		**5.54**

In these rather simplified examples, both blends have the same average age of 5.5 year. The second of the two would be a more 'consistent' blend, with more complexity.

A TYPICAL 10 YEAR OLD BLEND PRODUCED IN 2008			
Year	Age of each component (years)	% of each component	Proportion of final blend
2005	3	4	0.12
2001	7	25	1.75
1998	10	55	5.50
1995	13	10	1.30
1980	28	6	1.68
Average			10.35

that the wine meets The Institute's requirements. If it is rejected, the producer can request a retest or make adjustments to the blend and then resubmit samples.

When the wine has been accepted, an individually numbered seal will be issued for each bottle.

Once approved, the wine must be bottled within six months or be retested. It is possible to bottle part of a batch but the remainder, if kept for more than six months, will have to be retested.

Wine styles

Existing regulations describe the various wines styles as follows:

Wines with Indication of the Year of Harvest

Vintage (*Frasqueira/Garrafeira*) Wine of distinctive quality, produced from traditional varieties of the same harvest, using 100 % of the named grape and aged for a minimum of 20 years before bottling.

Colheita or **Harvest** Wine of good quality, obtained from recommended or authorised grapes of the same harvest and aged for a minimum of 5 years before bottling. To have the name of a grape on the label the wine must be produced from 100% of the named variety.

Solera Wine obtained from a single harvest, forming the basis of a batch from which a maximum of 10% may be bottled each year. An equal quantity of a wine of the same quality is used to fill the cask. A maximum of ten additions is allowed, then all remaining wine must be bottled.

Wines with Indication of Age

Wines are entitled to use age categories when their quality and characteristics comply with each particular style. The age categories allowed are 5, 10, 15, 20, 30 and over 40 years.

Reserve or Old (*Reserva*) Wine which complies in quality and characteristics with a 5-year-old style.

Old Reserve or Very Old (*Reserva Velha*)
Wine which complies in quality and characteristics with a 10-year-old style.

Special Reserve (*Reserva Especial*)
Wine of distinctive quality, which complies with the characteristics of a 10-year-old style.

Other wines
Selected or Finest (*Seleccionado*)
Wine of good quality, aged for a minimum of 3 years, a sample of which has been approved for a wine of this style.

Rainwater Wine of good quality, with a colour between 'gold' and 'medium gold', a Baumé degree of 1–2.5, a sample of which has been approved for a wine of this style.

Modified wine From 2002, the sale of bulk wines was banned. However, wine may still be sold and exported for use in the food industry, mainly to France and Germany. This wine is usually sold in containers of 25,000 litres and is 'modified' by the addition of salt (10gm/litre) and pepper (40ml/hL

TERMINOLOGY	
With respect to the designations for the degree of richness, the following terms are used:	

Style	Baumé
Extra Dry (*Extra Seco*)	below 0.5
Dry (*Seco*)	below 1.5
Medium Dry (*Meio Seco*)	1.0 – 2.5
Medium Sweet (*Meio Doce*)	2.5 – 3.5
Sweet (*Doce*)	above 3.5

Instituto do Vinho, do Bordado e do Artesanato da Madeira, IP

pepper essence). Sometimes, at the request of the customer, the wine is modified by the addition of salt only.

Madeira without additives
Smaller quantities of non modified wines may be sold to the confectionery industry. This is sold in containers of 220 litres. The wine must have a certificate from the importer, stating that it will not be bottled and sold.

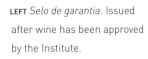

LEFT *Selo de garantia*. Issued after wine has been approved by the Institute.

Bottling

Producers may bottle their wines once they have received approval from The Institute. All companies have modern bottling lines, with the exception of Barros e Sousa, where they still bottle by hand.

The Institute must approve the labels used. Checks will be made, to ensure the labels meet EU standards. The label must include the name of the region (Madeira), the producer's company name, the brand name, the alcohol content (abv), and the volume. Where appropriate, the level of sweetness and the grape variety will be stated. Some labels may require extra information if the wine is to be exported to certain countries.

Automated bottling

A fully automated bottling line is a technical masterpiece. The stages of bottling include removing bottles from a pallet, rinsing and sterilising them,

Bottling by hand

At Barros e Sousa, bottling is carried out by hand. The bottles are sterilised and then filled individually, before being sealed using a hand corking machine. Labels are then individually stencilled onto the bottles. Such operations have been carried out in a similar way since the company was founded in 1922.

Edmundo Olim, one of the owners, filling a bottle from cask.

Edmundo Olim using a corking machine.

ABOVE 12 bottles being removed from the bottling line, to pack into cases.

filling, corking or capping, fixing seals and capsules, and labelling. The bottles are then packed in cartons. Some of the best wines will be individually packed.

Each stage of the operation is carefully monitored. The occasional breakdown provides a little excitement in an otherwise dull and routine process!

ABOVE Checking the bottling line, to ensure smooth running.

Chapter 6
Storing and Serving

Storing

Although Madeira wine is very robust and long lasting, it does, like all wines, need to be carefully stored, in order to enjoy it at its best.

The unique character of Madeira wines is due to the prolonged exposure to oxidation during the aging process and the high levels of alcohol and natural acidity. This makes it a wine of great longevity. Madeira has been kept for 150 years or more and found to be in excellent condition.

At Sotheby's in 2007, single bottles of Blandy's 1792 Bual sold for £828, £943 and £1012 respectively. More recently, in September 2009, Christie's sold some 'Fine Old Leacock Madeira', which included 1825 Madeira Seco for £650 (12 bottles), Saint John Vineyard 1927 Sercial for £240–£260 (3 lots of 6 bottles). They also sold Cossart Gordon 1860 Sercial Solera for £650 (6 bottles). Such prices indicate that the purchasers expect the wine to be in very good condition.

Bottles should be stored upright. Unlike table wines, they do not need to be stored horizontally because they have already been oxidised and so will not be harmed by contact with the air. If stored horizontally, the wine may destroy the cork and leak out.

There seems to be general agreement among the producers that Madeira wines should be stored at approximately 18–20°C, although Ricardo Freitas (Barbeito) says it should not exceed 18°C. Once opened, the wine can, if the temptation is resisted, be drunk over a very long period of time, as it will not deteriorate.

ABOVE Wines stored in tasting room at Barros e Sousa.

OVERLEAF Fruit and vegetable market in Funchal.

If wines are kept for many years, the corks may need to be replaced. Producers' opinions seem to vary about the time scale, from 8 years to 20+ years. Clearly, it will depend on the quality of the corks and the way in which the wines have been stored. A member of The Institute must be present at the producer's cellar when bottles are re-corked.

Serving

Some thought should be given to maximising the enjoyment of the wines by serving at suitable temperatures, using appropriate glasses. Madeira wines can be enjoyed with a range of foods.

Temperature

As with table wines, there are no fixed rules about serving temperatures. However, if the wine is cooled too much, the flavours will be masked.

Juan Teixeira, winemaker at Justino's recommends: Dry 9–11°C; medium dry 12–14°C; medium sweet 15–18°C; sweet 18–20°C; very old wines 18–20°C.

Francisco Albuquerque, winemaker at the MWC, recommends serving dry wines at 14°C and others at 17°C. He recommends opening the bottle early, up to 2 days before drinking, to get rid of any bottle aromas. He says "great care should be taken with very old wines".

Luis D'Oliveira recommends serving at 18–20°C, but "3-year-old and 5-year-old dry wines may be a little cooler".

Ricardo Freitas (Barbeito) recommends serving dry and medium dry wines at 14°C and medium sweet and sweet wines and Malmsey at 16°C. He points out that the temperature will often have increased by 1–2°C between serving and drinking. He suggests opening older wines and decanting them "well before" drinking.

Ivo Couto, winemaker at Borges, recommends serving all wines at 18°C and decanting old wines.

Luis Pereira, winemaker at Henriques & Henriques, suggests serving dry and medium-dry wines at 14°–16°C and medium-sweet and sweet at 16°–18°C.

Glasses

Like all wines, Madeira will benefit from being served in glasses that have a fine rim, which will throw the wine onto the tip of the tongue. Glasses should taper in towards the top, which will concentrate the aromas. They should be large enough to hold the required amount of wine plus an equal space above.

Food and wine pairings

As with all wines, it is a personal choice whether to drink them with or without food. If with food, the choice again is very personal. Readers may enjoy some of the following suggestions.

ABOVE Preparing for tasting at D'Oliveira.

Sercial and Dry With their clean, crisp acidity and subtle fruit and nut flavours, they can be drunk chilled as an aperitif. They can also be enjoyed with many fish and seafood dishes.

Verdelho and Medium-Rich/Dry They are aromatic, softer, lightly caramelised but still with the characteristic acidity of Madeira wines, and can be drunk chilled as an aperitif. They can also be enjoyed with cream soups and pâtés.

Bual and Medium-Rich/Sweet They are still relatively sweet, with flavours of vanilla, raisins and butterscotch. They can be a good accompaniment to lighter desserts or hard cheeses.

Malmsey and Rich/Sweet This is the sweetest style, with caramel, honey and raisin flavours and can be enjoyed with rich fruit cake or as a dessert wine. They are full flavoured and concentrated enough to accompany even the richest chocolate puddings.

and island blue cheese – Danish Blue, Roquefort, Stilton or Gorgonzola.

Medium Sweet Harmonious with fresh tropical fruits, dried fruits, cakes and fruit pies. Boal with aged cheese, soufflés, cheese or berries, butter cookies, milk chocolate, praline, petit fours, cream cakes and honey cake.

Medium Dry Excellent as an aperitif, combines perfectly with olives, roasted almonds and dried fruits, consommé, cream soups, onion soup gratin, serrano ham or smoked game, mushrooms stuffed with garlic, foie gras and pâtés .

Dry Excellent as an aperitif. It goes well with olives, roasted almonds, canapés of smoked salmon or caviar. It also pairs very well with smoked fish such as salmon, swordfish, tuna, or with seafood, sushi, fish mousse, fresh sheep and goats' cheeses. It can be enjoyed as a long refreshing drink with tonic water.

The Institute

Dry Excellent as an aperitif, this wine goes well with olives, roasted almonds, caviar or smoked salmon snacks. It goes equally well with fish such as swordfish, tuna, black scabbard, or

CHAPTER 6 STORING AND SERVING

Producers' recommendations

As the wines from different producers differ in style, aroma and flavour, each producer was asked for recommendations for food to partner their wines.

At D'Oliveira, visitors to the lodge are always offered some *Bolo de Mel* (honey cake) to accompany sweet wines. Luis D'Oliveira recommends pairing his wines with snacks.

At Borges, the winemaker suggests dry wines as an aperitif, and medium dry, medium sweet and sweet with cheeses and pâtés.

The following lists and tables show the pairings suggested by Barros e Sousa, Barbeito, The Institute, Henriques & Henriques, Justino's, and MWC.

Barros e Sousa

Sweet Combines with tropical fruits, dried fruits, walnuts and hazelnuts, dried fruit and cake, fruit tarts, honey cake, cookies of butter, milk or dark chocolate, praline and petit-fours, Portuguese cheeses – *Serra, Serpa, Azeitão, Rabaçal*

with seafood, sushi, fish mousse and cheeses made from sheep or goats' milk. It is refreshing as a long drink with tonic water, lemon and ice.

Semi Dry Excellent as an aperitif, it combines perfectly with olives, roasted almonds and dried fruits, consommé, onion au gratin soup, smoked ham or smoked game meats, wild game terrines, cottage cheese, stuffed mushrooms or mushrooms with garlic, foie gras and other pâtés.

Medium Sweet A perfect combination with fresh tropical fruits, dried fruits, cakes and fruit tarts. A young Boal combines with soft cheeses and an old Boal with ripe cheeses, cheese souffles or wild berries, butter biscuits, milk chocolate, petit fours, cream cakes and honey cake (*bolo de mel*).

Sweet Partners tropical fruits, dried fruits, nuts, cakes with dried fruits and fruit tarts, honey cake (*bolo de mel*), butter biscuits, dark or milk chocolate,

pralines, and petit-fours. It is equally elegant and combines very well with Portuguese cheeses like those from *Serra, Serpa, Azeitão*, that of *Rabaçal* and from the *Ilha*, and likewise with blue cheeses like Danish Blue, Roquefort, Stilton or Gorgonzola.

Henriques & Henriques
Monte Seco A light, pale, dry aperitif wine, which is particularly delicious chilled or on the rocks or as a long cool drink with tonic. It is also excellent with smoked salmon, other smoked fish, cured or smoked ham or cured duck or goose breast.

Special Dry An excellent aperitif, which can also be enjoyed chilled.

Medium Dry An aperitif or an ideal accompaniment for consommés, pâtés, particularly pâté de foie gras, cheeses or cakes. A very good all purpose wine.

Rainwater A pale, soft, medium dry wine. Its aroma and flavour are very delicate. It makes an excellent aperitif.

Medium Rich Delicious as a dessert wine or with such fruits as peaches, pineapples or fruit salads, chocolate, rich cakes and indeed with fresh strong

LEFT A glass of Sercial is an excellent accompaniment to salmon and asparagus.

83

SERVING

cheeses such as Roquefort or Stilton and other savouries, with coffee and as a digestif.

Full Rich A dark, full bodied, very fruity, luscious, fragrant and very rich sipping wine. It is to be savoured as a dessert wine, with rich foods, chocolate, petits-fours, with coffee and as a digestif.

Barbeito

Ricardo de Freitas is very keen to experiment with pairings of food with Madeira wines. He described some of his "most recent and surprising discoveries":

Strawberries with 10-year-old Boal; Oysters on ice with 10-year-old Sercial; Caramelised oranges and vanilla biscuits with 20-year-old Malvasia.

The following are taken from charts he has produced, showing pairings described as an "excellent match":

10-year-old wines

Sercial as an aperitif (with salted almonds/olives), or with French onion soup, game terrine (especially with onion marmalade), air dried

ham, and roast game (with caramelised vegetables).

Boal with duck or goose liver pâté, creamy blue cheese, mature Cheddar or other hard cheeses, crème caramel (or crème brûleé), *bolo de mel* (honey cake), Christmas cake, hot sponges (treacle, lemon, orange), ginger cake/parkin, or as a digestif (with nuts and dates).

An example of a
Barbeito Madeira Supper

Stuffed Mushrooms with
Parmesan Bread
Barbeito Sercial 10-years-Old

Welsh Rarebit
Barbeito Single Harvest 1997

Fruitcake with
Wensleydale Cheese
Barbeito Boal Single Cask 1999

Caramelised Oranges
With Vanilla Biscuits
Barbeito Malvasia 20-Years-Old

Coffee
Barbeito Verdelho 1981

RIGHT Ricardo de Freitas also organises suppers with Madeira wines paired with each course.

Malvasia with hard blue cheeses, mature Cheddar or other hard cheeses, apple tart with crème anglaise, treacle tart (or pecan pie), sticky toffee pudding, fruit cake (with Richard III Wensleydale) or as a digestif (with nuts and dates).

Justino's

Justino's has produced charts of suggested food and wine pairings. Selections from these pairings are shown below. Highly recommended pairings include:

Sweet

3-year-old with dried fruits, honey cake, desserts including coffee, as a digestif or with coffee

5 and 10-year-old Malmsey with butter biscuits, dark chocolate, fruit cake, honey cake, coffee desserts, strong flavoured cheeses and as a digestif or with coffee

ABOVE A sweet Madeira is the perfect partner for yoghurt cake.

Medium Sweet

3-year-old with dried fruits and tropical fruits.

5 and 10-year-old Bual with dried fruits and pralines, petit fours and soft and medium hard cheeses.

Medium dry

3-year-old with dried fruits.

5-year-old Verdelho with canapés or dried fruits.

10-year-old Verdelho with ham, delicate white meats or smoked game.

Dry

3-year-old as an aperitif or with dried fruits.

5 and 10-year-old Sercial with dried fruits, grilled or smoked fish.

10-year-old Sercial with ham or delicate white meats.

FOOD AND MADEIRA WINE PAIRINGS												
	3 Year Old Wines				5 Year Old Wines Harvest				10 & 15 Year Old Wines – Colheitas			
	Dry	Med Dry	Med Sweet	Sweet	S	V	B	M	S	V	B	M
Aperitif	x	x			x	x						
Digestif			x	x			x	x				
Consommé		x				x						
Soups & Creams		x				x						
Starters with Mayonnaise	x	x			x	x						
Starters of Indian Cuisine	x	x			x	x						
Dried Fruits	x	x	x	x	x	x	x	x	x	x	x	x
Milk Chocolate		x		x		x	x	x		x		x
Dark Chocolate								x		x		x
Pralinés		x		x			x	x		x		x
Petit Fours		x		x			x	x				
Dried Fruit Cakes		x		x			x	x				
Cream Cakes		x		x			x	x		x		x
Honey Cake		x					x	x		x		x
Chocolate Mousse		x						x		x		x

X = recommended. **S** = Sercial; **V** = Verdelho; **B** = Bual; **M** = Malmsey.

MWC

Francisco Alberqueque has produced a chart of pairings of Food and Madeira wine, part of which is produced above.

Also recommended is vintage Madeira with aromatic tobacco, cigars, cigarillos, or a pipe.

Further pairings

Américo Pereira, the commercial director of Diogos' wine shop in Funchal, is very involved in the promotion of Madeira wines to pair with food and works with chefs in

ABOVE Some of the food and wine parings suggested by Francisco Alberquerque.

many countries. Recently, with chef Momo Abane, he prepared a dinner for Rádio Televisão Portuguesa – RTPN – selecting a Verdelho Madeira for each course.

Américo Pereira is keen to point out that it is important, when planning menus, not only to consider the sweetness of the wine, the age and the grape variety but also the style of wine made by each producer.

Choupana Hills – Resort & Spa

AMUSE BOUCHE
Sashimi & Tartar of "Ceviche" Tuna fish
Avocado salad with tomato & green apple
&
Cossart Gordon Colheita 1998
Verdelho Single Harvest

STARTER
Smoked Cod Fish with Mango Rougail
Tomato cream Soup & crackling smoked ham
&
Barbeito Verdelho Frasqueira 1981
Bottled in 2005

MAIN COURSE
Veal Filet Mignon glazed and roasted with Foie Gras,
Baked Pear & Truffle "Jus"
Autumnal filo pastry with wild Mushrooms
&
D'Oliveiras Verdelho Frasqueira 1966
Bottled in 2007

DESSERT
Toasted Madeira Honey Cake "Millefeuilles"
Dried fruits & pistachio sauce
&
Cossart Gordon Verdelho Frasqueira 1934
Bottled in 1986

Nespresso & Petit Fours

CREATED BY: Chef Momo Abane, Américo Pereira e Ricardo Henriques

FOR: Rádio Televisão Portuguesa – RTPN
"Hora de Baco"

Chapter 7
Tasting

Tasting Madeira Wines

The pleasure of tasting and assessing Madeira wines is due to an array of factors, particularly the dramatic range and diversity of styles. Madeiras can be hugely complex.

Unlike table wines, Madeiras tend not to retain the primary fruit aromas and flavours, but show secondary and tertiary characteristics due to the fermentation and aging processes. The warming and oxidation during the aging process give aromas and flavours not experienced in table wines and other fortified wines.

The method of tasting Madeiras is that used for all serious wine assessment. The tasting sequence is: appearance; nose; palate; conclusions. These will be described in turn.

Appearance

Although appearance encompasses many aspects including clarity and depth, it is the colour in particular that warrants detailed examination.

Colour There is a notable colour range for different Madeira wines, depending on the grape variety, the vinification process, residual sugar content, the age and in some cases the addition

BELOW 1977 Terrantez, showing 'greenish' rim characteristic of old wines.

ABOVE From left to right; Blandy's 10-year-old Sercial, Verdelho, Bual, Malmsey, showing graduation of colour.

LEFT. Blandy's 5-year-old (*left*), 10-year-old (*centre*), and (*right*)15-year-old Malmseys.

LEFT The author examining the aromas of a 10-year-old Malmsey.

LEFT The author examining the aromas of a 10-year-old Malmsey.

Nose

The nose of a wine should be examined for cleanliness, intensity and aromas. Aromas may be considered in three basic groups: primary, secondary and tertiary.

Primary These are aromas that derive from grapes, and usually remain unchanged by fermentation and maturation. For example, many lovers of a wine made from Cabernet Sauvignon like the blackcurrant primary aromas of this variety.

Secondary These aromas are the result of fermentation and distinguish wine from fruit juice! A wine made from Cabernet Sauvignon smells of wine, not blackcurrant juice.

Tertiary At times incredibly complex, these aromas are the result of maturation and particular production techniques, such as heating of wines. They are especially prominent in Madeira wines.

Aromas and flavours

The unique production process for Madeira wines gives rise to a vast number of aromas and flavours. Unlike table wines there will be aromas and

of caramel. This means that colours of the same style of wines from different producers can be quite different.

The following list may be useful as a guide to the range of colours seen in Madeira wines:

pale gold – gold – amber – tawny – walnut – mahogany

The range above is not exhaustive and the taster may use many other individual colour descriptors. The colour tends to darken with sweetness, age and the addition of caramel. One feature that helps to distinguish older Madeiras is a 'greenish' rim.

flavours associated with the special aging process, during which oxidation takes place. Heating of wines during the *Estufagem* or natural heating in the *Canteiro* processes gives rise to caramelisation of the sugars.

Common aromas and flavours include:

Herbaceous – fresh cut grass, tea, sweet peppers.
Wood – pine, eucalyptus, vanilla, turpentine, varnish.
Sugars – caramel, toffee, molasses, chocolate, coffee, honey, smoke.
Microbiological – yeast, mushroom, lactic (butter, yoghurt).
Dried fruits – orange, apricot, prune, greengage, raisin.
Nuts – almond, walnut.
Spices – pepper, cinnamon, nutmeg, cloves, curry.

As the wines age, the aromas and flavours become more concentrated, intense and complex. The winemaker and blender must therefore decide the ideal time to bottle each wine.

Palate

On the palate, the taster detects dryness and sweetness, acidity, body, alcohol, flavours, intensity, concentration, and length of finish. It is the high acidity of Madeira that contributes to its unique style and incredible longevity.

Acidity A most important feature of Madeira wines is the acidity. In young dry wines, particularly Sercial, this can be very high. The following list provides a guide to the range of acidity levels of Madeira:

piercing – high – vigorous – brisk – moderate – fresh – tangy

It is the natural acidity that allows wines with very high residual sugar – 100^+gm/litre – to remain balanced. This balance is most important. If the acidity is too low, the wine can taste 'syrupy' and 'sticky'; if very high, the wine can taste sharp and acidic. The acidity is retained in very old wines, thus enabling them to remain in balance.

Sotolon, a sugar lactone (3-Hydroxy-4,5-dimethylfuran-2(5H)-one)$(C_6H_8O_3)$, is a very important volatile compound formed during the long heating process of maturation of Madeira wines. It is detected on both nose and palate and gives rise to a range of aromas and flavours. In low concentrations they include maple syrup, brown sugar, burnt sugar and caramel. As the concentration increases they include figs and dried fruits. At high concentrations Sotolon gives rise to curry-like aromas.

Sotolon has also been detected in Vin Jaune, sherries aged under flor and some wines made from botrytised grapes.

The following is a general description of the four main wine styles:

Malmsey/Malvasia (Rich) wines are the sweetest with rich honey, raisin and caramel flavours. They retain a natural high natural acidity, which balances the sweetness.

Bual/Boal (Medium-Rich) wines are drier, but still relatively sweet. They show nutty, vanilla characteristics, with the tangy, raisiny fruit and have a long butterscotch finish.

Verdelho (Medium-Dry) wines are aromatic, showing hints of caramel flavours and the characteristic Madeira wine acidity.

Sercial (Dry) wines still retain moderate amounts (25–60 gms/L) of residual sugar. They are clean and crisp, often showing mineral tones, with subtle fruit and nut flavours. The acidity is high and can be piercing in young wines.

The four descriptions above refer to wines made from the four main recommended white grape varieties. It is important to bear in mind that the predominant grape variety used for

As the wines are aged, the production of sotolon increases adding to the intensity and complexity of aromas and flavours. The formation of sotolon depends on the sugar content of the wine and the length of the aging process.

Conclusions

After considering appearance, nose and palate, the taster will be able to draw conclusions about the quality, readiness for drinking and other factors including possible food pairings.

The characteristics of Madeira wines

Attempting to describe the characteristics of Madeira wines is extremely difficult, because taste is such an individual experience.

Madeira wines is the approved red grape Tinta Negra. Many wines made from this grape are aged in *Estufas* and tend to be bottled as 3 and 5-year-old wines. The wines are labelled in terms of sweetness: dry; medium-dry; medium-rich and rich. The grape variety is not specified. They do show some of the characters described above but tend to be less complex and more straightforward. However, there is a growing interest in producing older wines from Tinta Negra (*see* Chapter 12).

The impact of age upon taste

Below is a description of some of the general characteristics of 3 to 10-year-old wines.

3-year-old (current) wines

These wines can exhibit fruity characteristics. There is often an underlying 'caramel' flavour and spiciness. Wines of this age, are, relatively speaking, very young and have not had time to develop the intensity and complexity present in older wines. Nevertheless, they can provide the drinker with much enjoyment.

5-year-old wines

The wines tend to develop more intensity and complexity of aromas and flavours. The descriptions below refer to the four main noble grape

varieties, but it must be borne in mind that many 5-year-old wines are also made from Tinta Negra.

Sercial is the palest and driest, with very fresh, sometimes high acidity. They often have slightly 'nutty' aromas and citrus/dried orange peel flavours. The wines do not exhibit 'big' flavours.

Verdelho wines tend to be darker in colour, medium dry, with moderate to high acidity. Sometimes there seems to be a 'metallic' sensation from the acids.

Bual wines can be quite dark (mahogany) in colour, are medium sweet and display aromas and flavours of smoke, caramel, dried and crystallised fruits.

Malmsey wines are often dark in colour. On the nose and palate they tend to be rich and sweet, with caramel and dried fruits.

Older Wines

From around 10 years, wines tend to lose their varietal differences and are recognised by the tertiary characteristics and their sweetness. The concentration and intensity of aromas and flavours increase with age. Flavours include nuts, spices, dried fruits, caramel, coffee, dark chocolate.

Tasting notes

The following is a selection of extracts from producers' and UK agents' tasting notes for their wines. Readers will note there are similarities but also differences between the same styles of wines made by different producers. It is the differences that provide such a wonderful diversity of Madeira wines.

3-YEARS-OLD MEDIUM DRY (TINTA NEGRA)
Barbeito
Nice deep amber-tawny colour, dominated by a nutty and straw character with a hint of brown sugar bouquet. Medium dry, suggesting some figs and dried apricot evolved in a fresh citric aftertaste.
Justino's
Translucent, with a shiny golden colour. A pleasant and intense aroma, with a sensation of freshness. Light with a long dry finish, with notes of cocoa, grape, apple and walnut.
Borges
Pale, medium orange gold, greening on the rim. Nutty aromas and a light flavour, firm acidity and medium length.
D'Oliveira
A slightly earthy nose with hints of caramel, pleasing nutty flavour.

5-YEARS-OLD SWEET/RICH (TINTA NEGRA)
Justino's
An excellent deep amber colour. Dried fruits on the nose. Elegant. Medium rich, soft, and balanced, with some complexity. A long and pleasant finish, with bittersweet chocolate notes and a hint of grapes.
Henriques & Henriques
Aging in oak casks has produced this intensely concentrated and rich wine, with a strong flavour of ripe fruit.
Barbeito
Light golden tawny colour, with a concentrated bouquet of vanilla, honey and hazelnuts, tasting of rich toffee and dried fruit flavours, with a fresh, clean orange acidity finish.
Borges
Golden brown. Bouquet of wood and nuts. Sweet, full bodied, balanced acidity.

10-YEARS-OLD SERCIAL

Henriques & Henriques

A dry wine, with a clean aroma showing its evolution. Medium body. This wine is reminiscent of brown spices, nuts and citrus peel. A complex wine with fresh acidity and with an extraordinary long finish.

MWC Blandy's

Pale, bright topaz colour with a golden tinge. Fresh with dry fruit, wood and citrus flavours with a fresh and nutty persistent finish.

Justino's

A light tawny golden colour. Fresh and dry on the nose, with hints of unripe walnut and hot honey. A delicate freshness on the palate. A medium length of flavour with a final hot, dry touch.

Barbeito

Pale, medium yellow and orange tones. Dry on the nose, fresh harmonious and clean aromas of dried fruits. Delicious with some citrus flavours. Very long and acidulous finish.

10-YEARS-OLD BOAL/BUAL

Henriques & Henriques

A wine with depth, medium body, acidity and sweetness. Lively and full with delicious flavours of caramel and toffee and a lasting aftertaste.

Justino's

An attractive and brilliant deep amber colour, with an intense, powerful bouquet of molasses and chocolate. Medium to full-bodied with complex flavours of dried fruits, spices and nuts. A medium to long finish.

MWC Blandy's

Clear, amber colour with tinges of gold on the rim. Superbly complex nose. Great intensity, revealing a bouquet of dried fruits such as figs and prunes, with notes of almonds and oak and subtle hints of toffee and vanilla spice. Sumptuous palate. Medium sweet and very smooth with a superb balance of coffee and fruit flavours with a clean and sharp acidity. Lovely persistent aftertaste.

Borges

Amber colour with a golden rim. Complex, wood and vanilla aromas. Medium sweet, good balance, long aftertaste.

15-YEARS-OLD MALMSEY

Henriques & Henriques
Brilliant amber colour with light golden shades. Complex aroma, a light 'toast', dried fruits and honey. Rich flavour, mellow and full-bodied, of raisins and other dried fruits. A nice finish.

MWC Blandy's
Clear, amber colour with a golden rim. Characteristic, complex, good intensity, strong bouquet of dried fruits (fig, prunes, almonds), wood and vanilla. Medium sweet, smooth, good balance, long and exuberant aftertaste, full-bodied and warm.

MWC Cossart Gordon
Lovely chestnut colour with a fine golden rim. Characteristic Madeira bouquet of dried fruits, toffee, vanilla and oak. Sweet, very rich, smooth and full-bodied. A long aftertaste with notes of spicy oak and dark chocolate.

Borges
Dark golden brown. Bouquet with complex dried fruits, vanilla and wood. Sweet, full bodied, complex, with a long finish of almonds.

SINGLE HARVEST AND COLHEITA

Justino's 1996 Sweet
Attractive in colour, with an elegant aroma with notes of walnut and caramel cake, slightly toasty. Pleasant on the palate, sweetness balanced by a vibrant acidity. A long finish, with suggestions of walnut and coffee. Good length of flavour, complex and with notes of baked apples and roasted walnuts.

MWC Blandy's 2001 Harvest
Amber colour with golden green reflections. Characteristic bouquet of Madeira with dried fruits, vanilla and wood. Rich and full bodied with notes of tea, toffee, spices and chocolate. Sweet and smooth on the palate, with a honeyed aftertaste.

Barbeito Single Harvest 1995
Light golden orange colour. Bouquet of dried fruits, orange peel and honey, also on the palate, finishing with a nice harmony between dryness and sweetness. Lovely texture, elegant, spicy and complex.

D'Oliveira Colheita Malvasia 1989
Intensely rich nose and a full rich mouthful of raisins and caramel. A powerful long finish and finely balanced acidity belying its relative youth.

ABOVE Preparing for The Institute annual Madeira tasting, London, 2008.

FRASQUEIRA (VINTAGE)

Henriques & Henriques Verdelho 1934
Brilliant, dark amber, dark gold and greenish shades. Aromatic, dried fruits, honey, dried figs, some 'toast'. Medium dry, full bodied with flavours of dried fruits, honey, velvety. Long finish and well balanced acidity.

Justino's Verdelho 1954
Medium deep amber with green rim. Very delicate, fruity, nose, almost flowery and refreshing bouquet. Broad and powerful on the palate. Nut, Marmite and toffee flavours. Rustic in style, almost bone-dry and austere. Good concentration, racy acidity with long finish.

Borges Boal 1977
A brownish tone with yellow nuances. Penetrating aromatic, complex aroma with touches of woodiness which transmit toasted almond, caramel and chocolate. A full-bodied wine, well structured and with a large concentration. Strong wood presence, with firm tannins.

D'Oliveira Boal 1977
Rich caramel on the nose, barley sugar and toasted nuts on the palate, with a long complex finish and finely balanced acidity.

Chapter 8
The Producers

Eight Producers

From the large numbers of producers in the past, today there are just eight, seven of which export their wines. As in many industries, there has been considerable consolidation and amalgamation of smaller producers.

Liddell has written in great detail about the large number of merchants on the island during the seventeenth to the twentieth century. He describes the many factors that caused fluctuations in the production and export of wines, which of course meant that the number of producers and shippers varied considerably during this period.

It is fascinating to read how these companies were formed, developed, and either stopped trading or were taken over or amalgamated and at the beginning of the twenty first century the number of producers is only eight. Of these, three

were established in the second half of the nineteenth century and the rest in the twentieth century. Some incorporate much older companies.

The following profiles of the eight producers describe their history, structure, production facilities and philosophies. These have been obtained directly from the companies during a series of visits. It will be seen that there is no single strategy on what constitutes the best Madeira wines. This leads to a broad diversity, even amongst this small number of producers.

It will be noted that there have been many initiatives and changes during recent years, which are contrary to a commonly held perception that Madeira producers are captives of the past.

At the present time, in contrast to other wine regions of the world, there seems no interest in growers producing their own Madeira wines for the market. The capital expenditure would certainly be onerous and, in any event, the arrangements with the existing producers seem to work to the benefit of all.

BELOW Bottles of various Madeiras. (*From left to right*) Barros e Sousa, Borges, Faria, Justino's, Henriques & Henriques, MWC Blandy's, D'Oliveira, Barbeito.

ABOVE Edmundo (*on the left*) and Artur Olim.

The company was set up in 1922 for Artur de Barros e Sousa by his uncle Dr Pedro Jose Lomelino. Dr Lomelino was fond of wine and had been buying small amounts of good Madeiras. Artur Barros had a daughter Virginia, who married Edmundo Menezes Olim. They had three sons, Artur, Edmundo and Rui. The company is now run by two of them, Artur Olim (winemaker) and Edmundo Olim (sales). Rui Olim was a 'sleeping partner', but has now sold his interest in the company to his brothers.

Compared with the other seven producers, Artur de Barros e Sousa is tiny, producing only 3–4000 bottles a year. Apart from harvest time, the two brothers carry out all the work. When winemaking starts, their six sons help, because, as Artur says, "it is heavy work".

Grapes are purchased in small quantities from growers around the island, mostly the same growers each year. They no longer purchase Tinta Negra, and only buy the white varieties, Sercial, Verdelho, Boal, and Malvasia.

2006 was unusual, when sufficient Malvasia grapes were purchased to make 4000 litres of wine, together with approximately 2000 litres each of Verdelho and Sercial. In 2007 and 2008, the total production was 4146 litres and 2437 litres.

A neighbour presses the grapes and the must, without skins, is fermented in casks, using natural yeasts. The small quantity of alcohol required, is purchased from the MWC.

All wine is made by the *Canteiro* method, as Artur believes in traditional methods, claiming he is too old to become involved in the "totally different world of technology". They only have one machine, an old pump, to pump the wines to the lofts.

One can't fail to be enchanted by this small and highly traditional producer.

Wines are not exported, but sold "around this table" to visitors and islanders.

Artur de Barros e Sousa Lda
Rua dos Ferreiros 109,
9000-082 Funchal
Madeira
Portugal

Tel: +351 291 220 6222
Email: *absl@netmadeira.com*
www.vinhosmadeira.com

During the early 1990s, many old *solera* wines were available, but these have been sold. There are still small stocks of old wines "of our father". Some of these are labelled with the style and quality, and others with the grape variety. The date and in some cases the variety, is unknown! It should be noted that these wines have been tested and approved by The Institute.

Currently, the company has approximately 60,000 litres of stocks in casks. These include Moscatel, Listrão, and Terrantez.

Artur is in favour of new regulations brought in during recent years, saying "it makes life easier".

Although suggestions are listed on the company's website, he says Madeira wines should not be drunk with food and comments "with food is table wine". He adds, with a smile, "I do not drink my wines, alcohol is not for me, I drink water or coffee".

HM Borges, Sucrs, Lda

The company was founded in 1877, by Henrique Meneze Borges. Initially he was a food importer and then started to purchase and build up a stock of old wines. He died in 1916, leaving two sons, João and Henrique and a daughter, Maria. In 1925 Borges purchased the company Adega Exportadora de Vinhos de Madeira.

Maria, HM Borges' daughter, married João Henriques Gonçalves, who merged his firm with Borges. In 1932, he bought the firm, but kept

ABOVE Helena Borges Fontes (*on the left*) and Isabel Borges Gonçalves.

the name. In the same year, the firm merged with Araújo Henriques & Co. Maria and João had two sons, Jorges and Fernando and a daughter.

Two cousins, who are the fourth generation of the family, now run the firm on a day-to-day basis. Isabel is the daughter of Jorges and Helena the daughter of Fernando. Other members of the family and the Araújo family are also shareholders. Ivo Couto, a winemaker for 30 years, joined the company six years ago. Altogether, there are now 14 employees.

The Araújo family owned vineyards that supplied the company with Verdelho grapes. Today, they still grow grapes but these are used for table wines not Madeira wines. With help from two agents, all grapes for Madeira wine are purchased from a number of growers especially in Câmara de Lobos and from the north of the island.

The company lodge in Funchal is an old flour mill, which they purchased in 1922. It houses all the winemaking equipment – presses, fermentation tanks, *Estufas* – storage and aging facilities, bottling line, a small laboratory and a visitors' reception and tasting room.

The company purchases an average of 200,000 kg of grapes per year. Tinta Negra is purchased from Estreito de Camara de Lobos, Sercial from São Vicente, Verdelho from Calheta, Boal from Campanário and Malmsey from São Jorge.

The current annual production is approximately 150,000 litres, 75–80% of this is 3 year old. The company holds stocks of approximately 1 million litres.

In addition to the Borges brand, the company also produces wines under the brands of Adega Exportadora de

HM Borges, Sucrs, Lda
Rua 31 de Janeiro, 83
9050 – 011 Funchal
Madeira
Portugal

Tel: +351 291 223 247
Email: *hmborges@mail.telepac.pt*

Vinhos de Madeira, JH Gonçalves and Araújo Henriques & Ca. The Adega brand is sold to Japan, the Gonçalves and Araújo brands are sold locally, and the main markets for the Borges brand are Sweden, Norway, Italy and the UK.

Annual sales are approximately 100,000 litres.

The company does not sell bulk or modified wine.

Although noted in the past for its old vintage wines, most of these have been sold. The oldest available wine is a 1940 Malmsey Solera. Now, 80% of the sales are 3 year old wines. 3 and 5 year old wines are made from Tinta Negra and 10 and 15 year old from Sercial, Verdelho, Boal and Malmsey. The company also makes single harvest wines and recently made a 40 year old Malmsey to celebrate the 500th anniversary of the city of Funchal. A full list of wines can be found at the end of the book.

The company has no interest in making table wines.

The company was founded 60 years ago and produces a large range of various alcoholic beverages such as rum, poncha, and many fruit based drinks including lime, passion fruit, and nectarine.

J Faria & Filhos, Lda
Travessa do Tanque, 85/87
9020 – 258 Funchal

Tel: + 351 291 742 935
Email: *jfariafilhos@sapo.pt*

Ten years ago, the company became involved with Madeira wines, in association with PE Gonçalves, who until 2002, produced and sold wines in bulk. Gonçalves buys in grapes and must and produces Madeira wines, both by the *Estufagem* and *Canteiro* processes.

The Faria company moved to its new premises in Funchal two years ago. It is quite an extensive, modern, five storey building, with room for a planned expansion, as involvement with Madeira wines increases.

The first wines produced were a sweet and medium dry 3 year old, made from Tinta Negra. Then the range was increased to include dry and medium sweet. There is now a 10 year old Tinta Negra and, from the 2008 harvest, it is intended to produce a 5 year old *Boal*.

Annual production was 238,437 litres in 2007 and 253,880 litres in 2008.

Sales started with the local market and the Portuguese mainland. Now the company exports to France. Total sales in 2008 were 180,000 litres.

The company plans to increase production and sales in the future. At the time of writing, the facilities for Madeira wine included storage for casks, a bottling line, and some very recently installed 50,000 and 60,000 litre stainless steel storage tanks. Future plans include the purchase of two 50,000 litre stainless steel *Estufas*, more storage tanks and oak casks, in order to have a total storage capacity of 600,000 litres.

At present, the company markets several brands: Faria & Filhos Lda and J Faria for Portugal and export markets; Zarco, Nau Santa Maria de Colombo and Pingo Doce, for the local market. Pingo Doce is also sold in Portuguese supermarkets.

Clearly the intention is to continue the partnership with PE Gonçalves and increase the range of wines produced. Possible new markets include Germany, UK and Latin America.

LEFT Luis Faria, Managing Director.

Henriques & Henriques, Vinhos, SA

ABOVE Luis Pereira, winemaker *(on the left)* and Humberto Jardim, CEO.

The company was established by João Joaquim Henriques in 1850. Two of his three sons, Francisco and João inherited the company. After his brother's death, João inherited the company and he invited two friends, Alberto Jardim and Carlos Pereira to join the company. Later Peter Cossart, brother of Noël Cossart, of Cossart Gordon joined. In his will, João left his three friends equal shares in the company.

Today, there are several shareholders, and the day-to-day business is run by the CEO Humberto Jardim and winemaker Luis Pereira, who is the nephew of Carlos Perreira. Following the death of John Cossart, son of Peter Cossart, early in 2008,

Humberto Jardim became president of the company.

In the early 1990s, with the aid of EU grants, the company moved from Funchal to two sites, a five storey building in Câmara de Lobos, and a 17ha site at Quinta Grande, Ribeira do Escrivão, at a cost of €5.5m.

The building at Câmara de Lobos houses a cask store, stainless steel holding and blending tanks, offices, a laboratory, a tasting room, and a visitors' reception area with shop.

The laboratory is well equipped and can measure abv, total extract, volatile acidity, total acidity, relative density, Baumé, Sodium, total SO_2, pH, colour and can check for tartrates after cold stabilisation.

At Quinta Grande is the company's vinification centre, with vinification tanks, storage tanks, presses, filters, stainless steel *Estufas* and a storage area for casks.

Henriques & Henriques is the only company that owns vineyards. It has 10ha at Quinta Grande, planted mainly with Verdelho, some Sercial and a small amount of Terrantez. The vines are planted on terraces that are at a height of 650–800 metres, and the planting is on the *Espaldeira* system. The company also has a vineyard of 1.0ha in Câmara de Lobos, which is planted with Tinta Negra, using the *Latada* system.

The company's vineyards only supply approximately 15% of their normal annual requirements of 800,000–900,000kg. The remaining 96% are purchased from growers around the island.

Six agents, two in the north and four in the south, help the company with the purchases.

Current production is 700,000–980,000 litres. This includes 300–400,000 litres sold as 'modified' wine.

Production includes a range of 3 and 5-year-old wines made in *Estufas* from

Henriques & Henriques, Vinhos SA
Avenida da Autonomia Nº10
9300-146 Câmara de Lobos
Madeira
Portugal

Tel: +351.291.941.551
Email: *heh@henriquesehenriques.pt*
www.henriquesehenriques.pt

Tinta Negra, and 10 and 15 year old wines made by the *Canteiro* process, from Sercial, Verdelho, Boal and Malvasia. The company also makes single harvest wines and has a small stock of older reserve and vintage wines. A complete list can be found at the end of the book.

The company's markets include France (mainly 'modified' wine), Germany, Sweden, UK, Denmark, USA, Canada, Japan, Belgium, British Virgin Islands, Italy, Netherlands, Ireland, Czech Republic, Greece, Australia, Dubai, Hong Kong, Iceland, Luxembourg, Spain and Gibraltar.

The company matures Madeira wine in casks belonging to an Irish whiskey company. The empty casks are then returned to be used for maturing whiskey.

Whilst many changes have taken place over the years and the company has excellent equipment and facilities, they are keen to maintain traditional methods. Consistency of styles and blends is extremely important.

LEFT Juan Teixeira, Winemaker and General Manager.

and is known as Justino's, Madeira Wines, SA.

In 1994/5, the company, with the aid of EU grants, built a new winery in a business park located in Cancela, Santa Cruz. This has improved the conditions in which the wines are made, in particular the vinification processes and aging. This large, modern and functional winery has been equipped so as to combine traditional methods with the most advanced technology available. By the end of 1995, the company had completed the move to Santa Cruz, from the centre of Funchal in Rua do Carmo, the site of the offices, warehouses and aging vats, and Rua do Ribeirinho de Baixo, where the vinification and bottling took place.

'Vinhos Justino Henriques, Filhos, Lda' was formed as a limited company in 1953, although it had been in existence since 1870 in Madeira as a private family company, when it was known as 'Justino Henriques'. This makes it one of the oldest producers and exporters of Madeira wine. Until the 1960s, family members owned the company.

Sigfredo Costa Campos, who purchased the company in 1981, developed markets in Europe, Brazil, the United States and Japan. In order to expand and modernise the company, he developed an association with one of the largest French producers and distributors of alcoholic beverages, La Martiniquaise. Sadly, Mr. Costa Campos died in 2008. Since the end of October 2009 the company has been totally owned by La Martiniquaise

An investment programme, which started in 2002, had a number of different objectives. These included improving the technology used to receive the grapes, the vinification process and increasing the storage capacity for wines aged in wood. It also involved improving the efficiency of the laboratory, in particular controlling the vinification process and quality control of the final product and increasing the production of wines in bottle. The existing bottling facilities were improved by installing two new bottling lines.

The company purchases grapes from approximately 800 growers each year, quantities ranging from approximately 120kg to 30,000kg, with an average of 2500kg. The grapes are mainly from Câmara de Lobos (Tinta Negra) and Estreito de Câmara de Lobos (Tinta Negra) (60%), São Vicente (Tinta Negra, Sercial and Verdelho), São Jorge (Malvasia) and Calheta (Boal and Verdelho) (40%). About 90% of the grapes purchased are Tinta Negra plus some Complexa and other red varieties and 10% are white varieties.

Annual wine production is approximately 1.6 million litres, of which 20–25% is exported as 'modified' wine for use in the food industry, mainly to France and Germany.

The company produces a range of 3, 5 and 10 year old wines from Tinta Negra and other red varieties, in dry, medium dry, medium sweet and sweet styles. The company's policy is to make dry and sweet styles but it also makes medium dry and medium sweet styles for customers who request them. It also makes 10 year old wines from Sercial, Verdelho, Boal and Malvasia, and some sweet, single harvest wines from Tinta Negra, Boal and Malvasia.

Justino's, Madeira Wines, SA
Parque Industrial da Cancela,
9125 – 042 Caniço,
Santa Cruz
Madeira - Portugal

Tel: +351 291 934 257
Email:justinos@justinosmadeira.com
www.justinosmadeira.com

A stock of older vintage wines is also available. A complete list can be found at the end of the book.

A new and interesting project for the company, is the production of wines from certified organic (Bio) grapes. During the 2008 harvest, the company purchased 15,101kg of organic Tinta Negra grapes from a grower in Estreito de Câmara de Lobos. From this, they have produced 11,300 litres of sweet Madeira wine. The winemaker has described the condition of the grapes as "excellent", with a potential alcohol of 10–12%. They were fermented in stainless steel at 28–30°C, with frequent pumping over for three days. All of the wine will be aged by the *Canteiro* process. Depending on how the wine evolves, it is hoped it will be bottled at 10 or 15 years old.

The company's principal markets include France, Germany, Poland, Austria, Switzerland, the Benelux countries, Spain, UK, Scandinavia, USA, Japan, Brazil and Canada.

JUSTINO'S, MADEIRA WINES, SA

The
Old
Blandy
Wine
Lodge

→

Museum | **Visits** | **Tastings**
Museu | Visitas | Provas

The origins of the Madeira Wine Company can be traced back to the foundation of The Madeira Wine Association in 1913. This was formed to promote Madeira wines in the international market and to improve their production and quality. In 1925, the well established family firms of Blandy's and Leacock joined the Association, followed some years later by Miles and Cossart Gordon. The Association was the largest producer and exporter of Madeira wines.

The name was changed to the Madeira Wine Company in 1981, by which time, the company had been reduced to a few of the original companies, with the Blandy family holding the controlling interest.

The Blandy family has played a leading role in the development of Madeira wine throughout its long history. They decided they needed a partner who could help develop the company's brands profile and strengthen sales and marketing worldwide. In 1989 the Blandy's invited the Symington Port company, producers of Port for four generations, to become a partner. Today, the company is jointly and entirely owned and managed by the Blandy family of Madeira and the Symington family of the Douro.

At present, the company has two premises in Funchal: The Old Blandy Wine Lodge in Avenida Arriga, and the Mercês Complex.

The Old Blandy Wine Lodge dates back to the 17th century. It houses over 8000hL of premium wines aging in the *Canteiro* process. The Lodge is a centre for visitors, with conducted tours of the aging lofts and a museum of winemaking equipment and old company documents. There are also tasting rooms with shops where the company's wines can be purchased and a wine shop, selling a range of wines and wine related items.

The Mercês Complex houses the production centre (winery) and offices, and was completely modernized in 2001/2002. This facility has two vinification lines with a total capacity to receive up to 130 tonnes of grapes per day. There are three bottling lines, one automated with a capacity of 6000 bottles/hour, one manual with a capacity of 1000 bottles/hour and an automatic line for miniatures. It also has a storage capacity of 50,000hL, including 14,000hL in wooden casks and vats and 7300hL in *Estufas*.

Annual production during the past five years has been approximately

LEFT The entrance to The Old Blandy Wine Lodge, tasting rooms and museum.

990,000 litres. In 2008, the company purchased approximately 850 tonnes of grapes, of which 650 tonnes were Tinta Negra and 200 tonnes white varieties. The company's sales represent approximately one third of the bottled Madeira wine market on the island and over half of the bottled export market worldwide.

The company's policy is to make all 3 year old wines from Tinta Negra and other red grapes, aging them in *Estufas*. All other wines, from 5 years and above are produced from Sercial, Verdelho, Bual, Malvasia and Terrantez and are aged by the *Canteiro* process.

Due to its history, the Madeira Wine Company has a rich portfolio of brands. Today the prominent three

ABOVE Display casks for MWC brands.

brands are Blandy's, Cossart Gordon and Leacock's. A small amount of wine is made for the Miles brand. The company has defined specific criteria to be used in the production of each wine, in order to give each brand its own profile.

The company's leading brand is Blandy's. Its wines are made with a slightly shorter fermentation than for the other brands, thus leaving more residual sugar, giving richer, more full-bodied wines. Blandy's is particularly known for extensive reserves of old vintage Madeira and for its famous Duke of Clarence Full Rich Madeira. In recent years, Blandy's has received many prestigious awards.

Cossart Gordon wines are slightly lighter and made with a slightly longer fermentation using grapes from grapes from higher, cooler vineyards, giving drier wines.

Leacock's wines maintain their traditionally rich style and are noted for Leacock's St John Madeira, while Miles have broken with Madeira Wine Company tradition and now offer customers 5 year old wines made from the Tinta Negra grapes. Miles wines tend to be contain more residual sugar.

In recent years, the company has launched three new innovative concepts; the *Harvest*; the *Alvada*; *Colheitas*.

The first, Blandy's Harvest 1994, was launched in 2000. This was the release of a young Single Harvest, at an affordable price for consumers. Aged in the *Canteiro* process, the wine remains for 6 to 8 years in oak casks in lofts in Funchal before being bottled. It displays concentration and complexity similar to 5 year old blends.

Two years later, in 2002, the company launched an innovative idea: the Alvada. Both the wine and the packaging were completely new to Madeira. The Alvada is a blend of 50:50 Malmsey and Bual, whereas traditionally Madeira wines have always been made from a single variety. The modern packaging has an elegant bottle with striking

Madeira Wine Company, SA
Rua dos Ferreiros, 191
9020-082 Funchal

Tel: +351 291 740 100
Email:
secmerces@madeirawinecompany.com

colours, thus showing Madeira in a totally new light.

The Harvest and Alvada were followed by the Cossart Gordon Colheitas. These are carefully selected from the many wines in the lofts and are aged from 10 to 18 years. They can be seen as 'baby vintages' and have considerable complexity and concentration. The range includes Tinta Negra, Sercial, Verdelho, Bual and Malmsey.

In 2009 Madeira Wine Company expanded the concept of Colheita to its flagship brand, Blandy's, presenting two Single Harvest Boals and two Single Harvest Malmseys. The Blandy's Colheitas are aged from 10 to 19 years and have been carefully chosen from the many casks maturing in the lofts. All bottles are numbered, the casks identified and the label bears the signature of a direct descendant of the founder of Blandy's.

The company also makes a comprehensive range of 3, 5, 10 and 15 year old wines, and vintage wines. A complete list can be found at the end of the book.

Pereira D'Oliveira (Vinhos), Lda

Pereira D'Oliveira (Vinhos) Lda is a Madeira wine production and export business. Founded in 1850 by João Pereira D'Oliveira , the company now incorporates five Madeira wine producers and exporters, all previously run by island families. The oldest of these dates back to the 1820s. The most recent, Adegas do Torreao Lda, founded in 1947, became part of the company in 2002.

Today the company is run by the founder's grandsons Aníbal and Luís and Aníbal's son Filipe, who joined the firm as winemaker in 1987.

ABOVE Filipe *(on the left)* and Luis D'Oliveira.

The headquarters of the company is a beautiful listed building in Funchal. It dates back to 1619 and was purchased in 1911. Records show that this superb building was the first secondary school in the country in 1837. It now houses the tasting and sales room and some large vats and barrels of maturing wines, some up to a hundred years old. Renovations to the building have recently been completed.

The recently purchased Adegas do Torreao building, adjacent to the MWC, is now the winery. When refurbishment is complete it will also have some tasting rooms that were previously *Estufas*!

During the 1960s and 70s, the family owned farms, with cattle, pigs, bananas, sugar and vines. The vines supplied 20–30% of the company's grapes. A decision was made in the late 1980s, to sell the farms and concentrate on the winemaking business. Since 2000–01, the company has purchased all its grapes from local growers. Tinta Negra is bought from Estreito de Câmara de Lobos and São Vicente, Sercial from Ponta Delgada, Verdelho from Seixal and São Vicente, Bual from Calheta, and Malmsey from São Jorge. The company is still able to source a small amount of Terrantez. The total amount purchased each year is 120–150 tonnes.

The company did not export much wine until the 1970s. Today they have a considerable stock of rare old wines, totalling about 1.5 million litres, built up over the years from the company's own wines and those of the companies it purchased. The oldest wine on the 2009 list is a Verdelho 1850.

The present production is approximately 150,000 litres per year.

Pereira D'Oliveira (Vinhos) Lda
Rua dos Ferreiros, No 107
8000-082 Funchal

Tel: +351 291 220 784
Email: *perolivinhos@hotmail.com*

This includes a range of 3, 5, 10 and 15 year old wines made from Tinta Negra and 15 year old and older wines made from Sercial, Verdelho, Boal, Malvasia and Terrantez. Wines up to 10 years old are made by the *Estufagem* process and wines of 15 years or older by the *Canteiro* process. The company also produces single harvest wines. A complete list can be found at the end of the book.

30–40% of the wines are sold on the island, mainly to visitors. Wines are exported to mainland Portugal, Austria, Belgium, Czech Republic, UK, USA, Canada, Japan and Russia.

Luis D'Oliveira makes it clear that he wishes to stay as a family business and to maintain the company's identity. They have never made Soleras or blends containing more than one grape variety and have no wish to do so. His aim is "to keep all casks full" and to continue to maintain stocks of old wines. He wishes to "invest in new technology but learn from the past".

The company is not interested in producing table wines.

The company was founded in 1946 by Mário Barbeito who, as an accountant for Companhia Vinicola da Madeira, was motivated to set up his own business. He had a modern outlook towards the future possibilities. His daughter Dona Manuela Freitas became involved in 1976, and took control of the company in 1985, when Mário Barbeito died. In 1991, two of her sons, Ricardo and Miguel, joined the firm and Dona Manuela retired in 1992.

In 1991, a joint venture was set up with Kinoshita International Company Ltd of Japan. Mário Barbeito had been selling wines to the owners of Kinoshita since 1967, and so by the time of the partnership between the firms, a good relationship had developed between the families over a 24 year period.

In 2004, José, Manuela's youngest son joined the company and her oldest son, Miguel, left. In 2007, Emanuel, Ricardo's other brother, joined the

ABOVE The Barbeito 'team' at the opening of the new winery in November 2008.

company. Ricardo de Freitas manages the firm on a day-to-day basis, in consultation with his brother. After meeting him for just a few minutes, it is clear what a dynamic person Ricardo is.

The brothers realised they could not compete with the larger companies, so the decision was made to create unique styles, with fresh fruity wines, using traditional methods. In 1991, the company stopped bulk sales and concentrated on quality rather than quantity. In order to produce cleaner wines with purer colours, it was decided to stop using caramel. They also decided to look towards the younger consumer. This seems to have worked. The traditional consumer also seems to like Barbeito styles, which Ricardo describes as having very fresh acidity and containing no caramel.

The company purchases grapes from approximately 135 growers each year. 50% of these families have been selling to the company for over 15 years.

In 2008, the company made a major change, moving premises from Funchal to a newly built winery at an industrial park in Câmara de Lobos. It houses state-of-the-art equipment, with two pneumatic presses; the only robotic lagar on the island; a range of stainless steel fermentation and storage tanks and *Estufas*. There is also storage space for wines to mature in cask.

The move involved an enormous amount of work but means that now all winemaking and most aging can take place on the one site. The company will keep its warehouse in Câmara de Lobos, where it is currently aging 80,000 litres of Madeira wine, but its other warehouses will be closed and the wines moved to the new winery. The Institute must supervise the removal of each cask.

The new winery was officially opened in November, when the partners from Japan and 150 guests attended. The winery has a visitors' centre with a tasting room.

In addition to a range of 3, 5 and 10-year-old wines, Ricardo de Freitas has produced single harvest, single cask and vintage wines. He also makes a range of wines for Fortnum & Mason (UK) and for The Rare Wine Company (USA). Details of the wines can be found at the end of the book.

Ricardo is very keen to pair his wines with food. During a visit, he told me of some of his 'discoveries' (*see* Chapter 6).

In March 2009, 50 Verdelho vines were planted on a small plot at the winery, for experimental purposes.

The company has no plans to produce table wines in the near future, although the new winery gives them the capacity to do so.

Annual production has been approximately 200,000 litres during the past 4 years. In 2008 it was 262,000 litres. Annual sales for the last two years have been 150–160,000 litres, with the main market Japan (77%). Other markets include Madeira, Australia, USA, UK, Norway, Switzerland, Belgium, Germany, France, Denmark and Italy.

Vinhos Barbeito (Madeira) Lda
Estrada da Ribeira Garcia
Parque Empresarial de Câmara
de Lobos – Lote 8
9300-324 Câmara de Lobos
Madeira
Portugal

Tel: + 351 291 761 829
Email: info@vinhosbarbeito.com.pt

VINHOS BARBEITO (MADEIRA), LDA

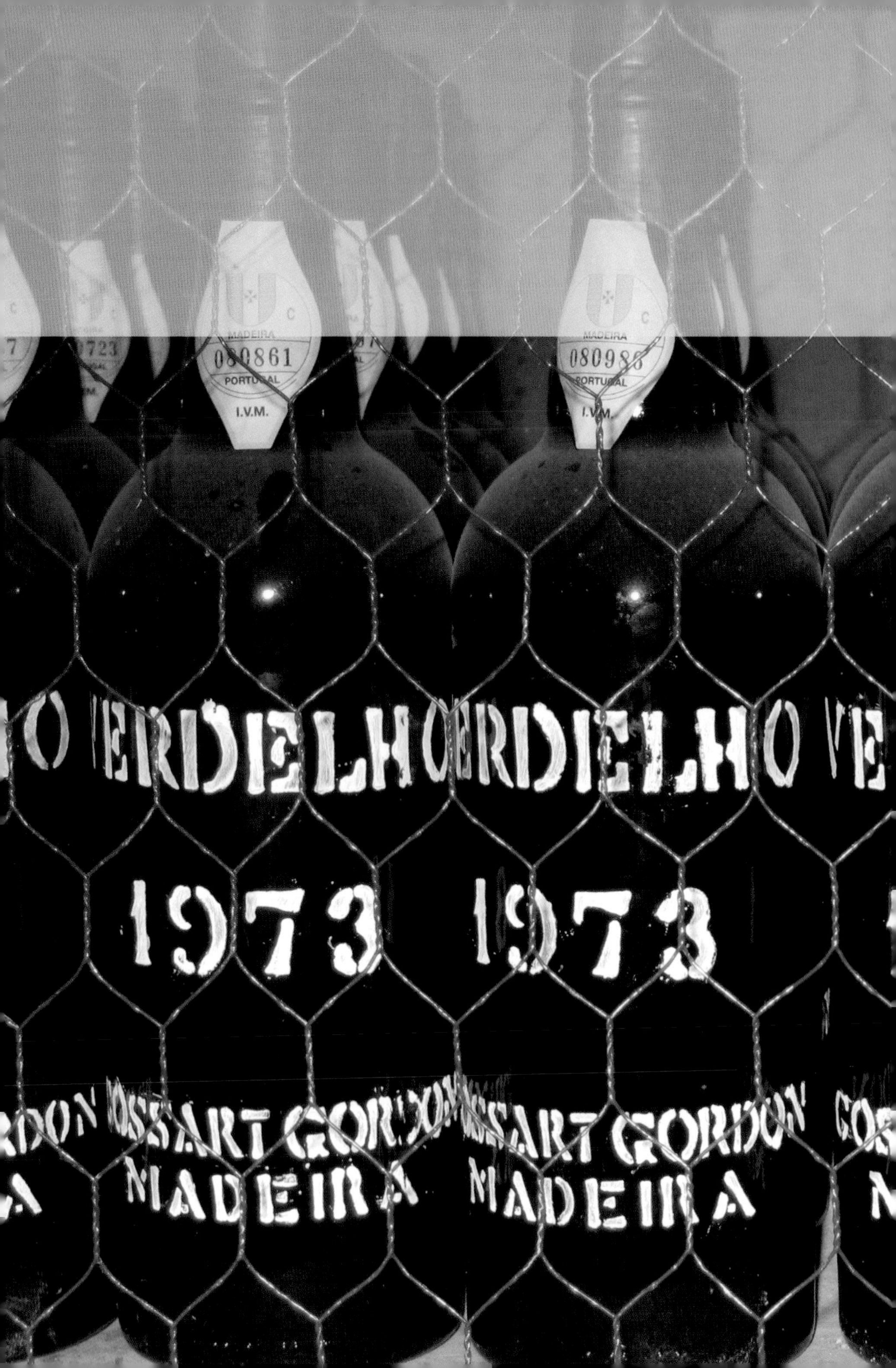
MADEIRA
080861
PORTUGAL
I.V.M.
1973
1973
MADEIRA
MADEIRA

Chapter 9
Commercialisation

ABOVE Tinta Negra grapes, ready to transport to the winery.

Production

This chapter looks at the trends in production and sales of Madeira wines for 2005–2009, analysing sales in terms of grape varieties, styles and ages. It also refers to the requirements placed on producers to maintain stocks of wine.

The average weight of grapes per year used for the production of Madeira wine in 2005–2009 was 4.1 million kg. This produced an average of 4.0 million litres of wine.

Over the five years, just 12% of the grapes used were Malvasia, Boal, Verdelho, Verdelho, Sercial and a very small amount of Terrantez. The remaining 88% was Tinta Negra and a small amount of other approved varieties.

Although Terrantez is grown in very small quantities, there has been an increase year on year between 2005–2009.

PRODUCTION OF MADEIRA WINE

Year	Grapes for Madeira Wine (kg)	Wine produced (litres)
2005	3,551,402	3,629,749
2006	4,410,693	4,313,966
2007	4,104,144	4,016,590
2008	4,668,895	4,349,573
2009	3,904,278	3,749,999

Instituto do Vinho, do Bordado e do Artesanato da Madeira, IP

PROUCTION OF MADEIRA WINE (KG)

Year	Malvasia	Boal	Verdelho	Sercial	Terrantez	Other permitted varieties	TOTAL
2005	205,209	196,793	43,665	97,886	479	3,007,370	3,551,402
2006	223,477	216,452	35,862	49,442	1,348	3,884,112	4,410,693
2007	197,118	209,004	42,835	54,258	1,454	3,599,475	4,104,144
2008	166,757	217,345	36,910	38,379	1,582	4,207,922	4,668,895
2009	170,827	112,367	35,305	38,220	2,206	3,545,354	3,904,278

Instituto do Vinho, do Bordado e do Artesanato da Madeira, IP

Sales

Only approximately 14% of Madeira wine is sold on the island. Exports are crucial to the success of the industry. In recent years, many new markets have opened up.

Markets

For the years 2005–2009 sales of Madeira wine have averaged 3.4 million litres. In recent years the number of markets, including the island of Madeira and mainland Portugal, has increased to 35. Approximately one third of sales is to France. Much of this wine is 'modified' and sold to the catering industry.

Most of the sales are to EU countries. Outside the EU, Japan and the USA are

SALES OF MADEIRA WINE BY MARKETS (LITRES)

	2005	2006	2007	2008	2009
Azores	960.00	1,236.00	1,200.00	963.00	270.00
Madeira	566,720.16	589,758.56	547,463.16	531,304.25	445,316.30
France	956,104.00	969,200.00	1,344,177.03	1,175,939.00	1,157,381.75
United Kingdom	324,700.25	377,270.25	354,762.75	242,919.50	305,722.50
Japan	225,250.60	208,604.60	195,277.80	205,283.70	219,983.50
USA	172,715.00	166,328.00	193,233.00	152,818.50	135,779.75
Germany	401,384.05	285,906.60	329,445.40	364,653.85	310,106.15
Belgium	171,675.00	146,730.50	172,485.40	150,170.50	175,468.00
Mainland Portugal	54,815.77	33,853.88	45,238.43	46,194.25	36,443.25
Holland	85,265.00	82,490.50	94,595.00	79,901.50	52,284.00
Canada	41,103.75	47,854.50	34,665.00	37,389.50	40,276.50
Denmark	55,752.00	80,479.00	86,623.50	49,411.50	45,266.50
Norway	10,620.00	14,505.00	11,826.00	11,180.50	22,033.50
Others	123,087.40	141,134.10	6,572,00	15,519.00	1,956.50
Others (EU)	16,879.50	26,365.65	1,240.50	763.50	1,116.00
Italy	6,461.25	5,625.00	8,252.25	7,974.75	1,858.50
Austria	20,959.50	22,813.25	31,464.00	31,803.00	29,355.00
Finland	27,277.50	24,225.00	34,746.75	28,234.50	34,332.00
Spain	8,613.00	9,769.50	6,735.75	5,427.00	9,987.00
Sweden	128,020.50	122,625.00	121,131.00	113,572.50	111,240.01
Poland			4,833.00	18,040.50	3,405.00

2009 MARKET SHARE IN %	
France	35.4
Island of Madeira	13.6
Germany	9.5
UK	9.3
Japan	6.7

the largest markets. In 2009, five markets accounted for nearly 75% of sales.

Indication of age

Based on the age of the wines, the largest volume sold is 'current' (3-year-old), which in 2009 accounted for 63.3% of sales. A further 24.4% of sales market was 'modified' wine and 'wine without additives'. The remainder was mostly 5- and 10-year-old wine.

SALES BY INDICATION OF AGE	
Current	63.3%
Modified	20.8%
Without additives	5.4%
Five-year-old	7.2%
Ten-year-old	2.0%
Colheitas and Vintages	0.9%

	2005	2006	2007	2008	2009
Czech Republic			3,703.50	1,863.00	2,496.00
Russia			2,344.50	2,133.00	378.00
Switzerland			104,969.00	96,793.00	93,974.70
Brazil			13,138.50	20,916.00	19,998.00
China			7,713.00	2,205.00	697.50
Cyprus			252.00	238.50	
Korea	139,966.90	167,499.75	3,975.00	2,214.0	1,266.00
Greece			2,547.00	1,671.75	1,689.00
Hungary			1,845.60	2,265.00	2,380.50
Ireland			1,890.00	3,357.00	1,764.00
Latvia			150.00	2,256.00	18.00
Luxembourg			5,847.00	5,744.10	5,287.50
Mexico			2,646.00	3,717.00	252.00
New Zealand			153.00	216.00	
Australia					1,506.00
Dubai					768.00
Macau					450.00
Singapore					900.00
Total	3,398,364.23	3,356,774.89	3,777,141.92	3,415,054.05	3,273,406.91

Instituto do Vinho, do Bordado e do Artesanato da Madeira, IP

SALES OF MADEIRA WINE BY INDICATION OF AGE

	2005	2006	2007	2008	2009
Madeira without additives	217,144.00	204,975.00	213,760.00	183,040.00	177,480.00
Modified	550,257.00	562,798.00	876,781.00	649,000.00	681,880.00
Current	2,222,538.98	2,163,798.93	2,253,962.29	2,202,818.69	2,073,653.13
5 years	269,171.25	295,672.01	285,446.38	242,717.21	234,829.43
10 years	86,980.50	81,841.45	94,138.50	85,572.05	64,004.25
15 years	12,406.00	14,893.00	14,131.50	12,532.50	12,590.85
20 years	327.00	687.25	363.00	607.50	258.75
30 years	48.75	200.25	762.75	805.50	42.00
40 years	189.75	186.75	300.00	125.25	47.25
Colheita and Vintages*	39,301.00	31,722.25	37496.50	37,835.35	28,621.25
TOTAL	3,398,364.23	3,356,774.89	3,777,141.92	3,415,054.05	3,273,406.91

Instituto do Vinho, do Bordado e do Artesanato da Madeira, IP

Sales (litres)		
	2008	2009
Colheitas	23,687.00	20,733.75
Vintages	14,148.00	7,887.50

*Separate statistics for production of Colheitas and Vintages have only been recorded since 2008.

Grape varieties

In terms of grape varieties, only a very small percentage of sales is wine made from the four main white varieties. In 2009 it was 5.7% of sales.

Malmsey	2.3%
Boal	1.4%
Sercial	1.2%
Verdelho	0.8%

The remainder (94.3%) was wine made from Tinta Negra and other recommended and authorised varieties. This wine is not labelled by variety but by styles of sweetness.

For 2009 sales were:

Rich	34.8%
Medium Dry	28.4%
Medium Rich	25.0%
Dry	6.1%

SALES OF MADEIRA WINE BY VINE VARIETIES						
			2005	2006	2007	2008	2009
Recommended and Authorised Varieties		Rich	927,769.10	1,228,804.38	1,262,433.80	1,285,238.	1,139,245.28
		Medium	558,727.69	449,250.34	831,022.93	598,256.09	818,131.55
		Medium Dry	11,142,019.33	840,839.05	804,126.81	980,314.61	929,958.02
		Dry	530,396.36	601,439.92	645,949.38	330,091.99	199,419.71
Malmsey			95,632.75	102,749.20	98,146.50	91,222.25	75,274.85
Boal			63,756.25	60,514.00	62,251.25	58,774.30	46,004.75
Verdelho			35,735.00	31,473.75	32,194.25	30,715.75	26,902.50
Sercial			44,327.75	41,704.25	41,017.00	40,440.20	38,470.25
TOTAL			3,398,364.23	3,356,774.89	3,777,141.92	3,415,054.05	3,273,406.91

Instituto do Vinho, do Bordado e do Artesanato da Madeira, IP

Age and grape variety

The table shows sales for the years 2005–2009, both by variety and age.

SALES BY AGE AND VARIETY			2005	2006	2007	2008	2009
Authorised and recommended vine varieties		Madeira without additives	217,144.00	204,975.00	213,760.00	183,040.00	177,480.00
		Modified	550,257.00	562,798.00	876,781.00	649,000.00	681,880.00
		Current	2,215,104.98	2,155,239.18	2,245,411.00	2,195,020.19	2,068,244.13
		5 years	148,615.75	171,737.51	174,049.88	142,094.86	144,461.18
		10 years	17,046.00	15,335.25	16,615.50	16,419.75	8,762.25
		15 years	1,572.75	2,634.75	201.00	192.00	354.00
		20 years	18.00	27.00	0.00	0.00	54.00
		30 years	0.00	72.00	0.00	126.00	0.00
		40 years	0.00	0.00	0.00	0.00	47.25
		Colheita & Vintages	9,154.00	7,515.00	8,614.00	8,008.75	5,471.75
MALMSEY		Madeira without additives	0.00	0.00	0.00	0.00	0.00
		Modified	0.00	0.00	0.00	0.00	0.00
		Current	6,768.00	8,550.75	8,100.00	7,686.00	5,400.00
		5 years	41,184.00	47,034.00	38,919.75	33,952.25	30,906.75
		10 years	25,414.25	27,120.45	37,841.50	26,683.65	19,298.25
		15 years	5,430.25	5,902.00	7,141.50	6,666.75	5,735.10
		20 years	291.00	508.50	363.00	607.00	204.75
		30 years	0.00	0.00	762.75	679.50	42.00
		40 years	0.00	0.00	0.00	125.25	0.00
		Colheita & Vintages	16,545.25	13,633.50	13,118.00	14,821.10	13,688.00

		2005	2006	2007	2008	2009
BOAL	Madeira without additives	0.00	0.00	0.00	0.00	0.00
	Modified	0.00	0.00	0.00	0.00	0.00
	Current	18.00	0.00	0.00	0.00	0.00
	5 years	31,595.00	31,360.50	30,975.75	26,310.75	22,676.25
	10 years	20,750.75	19,574.50	16,581.00	19,647.55	14,537.25
	15 years	3,379.50	3,905.25	3,881.25	3,659.25	3,450.00
	20 years	9.00	0.00	0.00	0.00	0.00
	30 years	21,75	108,00	0.00	0.00	0.00
	40 years	117,00	184,50	300.00	0.00	0.00
	Colheita & Vintages	7,865.25	5,381.25	10,513.25	9,156.75	5,341.25
VERDELHO	Madeira without additives	0.00	0.00	0.00	0.00	0.00
	Modified	0.00	0.00	0.00	0.00	0.00
	Current	18.00	9.00	0.00	0.00	9.00
	5 years	22,299.00	19,622.25	18,529.50	17,225.00	15,173.25
	10 years	8,713.50	7,458.75	8,839.00	9,086.25	7,954.50
	15 years	1,470.75	1,855.50	2,299.50	1,578.75	2,325.75
	20 years	9.00	150.75	0.00	0.00	0.00
	30 years	27.00	0.00	0.00	0.00	0.00
	40 years	18.00	0.00	0.00	0.00	0.00
	Colheita & Vintages	3,179.75	2,377.50	2,526.25	2,825.75	1,440.00
SERCIAL	Madeira without additives	0.00	0.00	0.00	0.00	0.00
	Modified	0.00	0.00	0.00	0.00	0.00
	Current	630.00	0.00	450.75	112.50	0.00
	5 years	25,477.50	25,917.75	22,971.50	23,134.10	21,612.00
	10 years	15,056.00	12,352.50	14,261.50	13,734.85	13,452.00
	15 years	552.75	595.50	608.25	435.75	726.00
	20 years	0.00	1.00	0.00	0.00	0.00
	30 years	0.00	20.25	0.00	0.00	0.00
	40 years	54.75	2.25	0.00	0.00	0.00
	Colheita & Vintages	2,556.75	2,815.00	2,725.00	3,023.00	2,680.25

Instituto do Vinho, do Bordado e do Artesanato da Madeira, IP

Reserves

Producers must keep a reserve stock of wines called the Normal Reserve (RN). This must be equal to the volume of exports for 18 months, based on the average for the past 3 years, up until 31st July each year.

Minimum purchase of grapes

Each harvest, producers must purchase a minimum quantity of grapes, sufficient to make a volume of wine equal to 75% of the volume exported in the previous 12 months up to July 31st. In the example shown, this would mean purchasing sufficient grapes in 2010, to make 247,500 (75% of 330,000) litres of wine.

If producers hold less stock than the Normal Reserve (*see* right) they will be required to purchase additional grapes to make up this deficit.

If producers hold stocks in excess of the Normal Reserve, a reduction in the minimum purchase of grapes is allowed. The maximum reduction allowed is 13%.

The chart shows the minimum quantity of wine to be made in 2010

STOCKS OF NORMAL RESERVE (RN)

Exports (litres)			Average (litres)	Normal Reserve (litres)
2007	2008	2009		(1½ x average)
300,000	300,000	330,000	310,000	465,000

The producer must therefore hold a stock (NR) of 465,000 litres of wine.

MINIMUM WINE QUANTITIES FOR 2010

	Producer A	Producer B
Production 2009	330,000	330,000
Average Production 2007–9	310,000	310,000
Normal Reserve (1.5 x Average 2007–9)	465,000	465,000
Stock	400,000	500,000
Replacement stock required	65,000	0
Excess of stock	0	35,000
Annual replacement (litres) (75% of 2009 production)	247,500	247,500
Minimum production 2010	247,500 65,000 **312,500**	247,500*

*Producer B holds stocks in excess of the Normal Reserve and would be allowed to make less than 247,500 litres of wine. The reduction allowed is based on one twelfth of the average production of the past three years (2007–9), which in this case is 310,000 divided by 12 = 25,833 litres. For every 25,833 litres above the Normal Reserve, a reduction of 1% is allowed.

MINIMUM PURCHASE REQUIRED

	Madeira Wine (litres)	Must (litres)	Grapes (kg)
Producer A	312,500	271,323	319,203
Producer B	244,147	211,976	249,384

Instituto do Vinho, do Bordado e do Artesanato da Madeira, IP

LEFT Casks on *Canteiro* in the loft at HM Borges.

by two producers, one holding less stock than the required Normal Reserve, the other holding more

Producer B has an excess of 35,000 litres and would therefore be allowed a reduction of 1.355%, reducing the minimum production from 247,500 litres to 244,147 litres.

The producers would therefore be required to purchase minimum quantities of grapes to meet the legal requirements.

LEFT Casks on *Canteiro* in the loft at HM Borges.

Chapter 10

Regulation and Development

RUA
FRANCISCO
FRANCO
"ESCULTOR"

IVBAM

Prior to 1979, the Junta Nacional do Vinho (National Wine Council) had the responsibility for coordinating and overseeing the wine industry. In 1979, the Autonomous Region of Madeira created the Madeira Wine Institute to take over these responsibilities. The Madeira Wine Institute was merged with the Madeira Tapestry, Embroidery and Handicraft Institute in June 2006, to form IVBAM, The Madeira Wine, Embroidery and Handicraft Institute (Instituto do Vinho, do Bordado e do Artesanato da Madeira, IP) – The Institute.

The Institute has responsibilities for "policies of coordination, support, valuation, and promotion of the vine, wine, embroidery and handicrafts of Madeira.

Within this organisation there are four Directorates: Vitiviniculture; Wine Sector Control and Regulation; Quality Support; Handicraft Services. There is also a Department that is in charge of the promotion and marketing of Madeira Wines and other traditional products such as embroidery.

Wine Sector Control and Regulation Directorate

This directorate has 13 full time members of staff. The work of the directorate is shared between the staff and some members have specific responsibilities. It involves checking the quality of wines,

collecting samples for analysis and tasting and checking the legal compliance of packaging and labelling. During the harvest, staff from other directorates assist with regulation and control work.

Although members of the directorate can carry out random inspections of premises used for production, processing, storage and trading of wines, most visits are made at specific times, during the harvest, winemaking, aging and bottling procedures. On average, depending on the size of the producer, visits by the directorate will average 1–3 per week.

The directorate is also involved in checking there are no breaches of regulations governing vineyards and wines. Possible breaches of regulations could involve: use of the designation of origin 'Madeira' for wines not from

ABOVE Institute staff (*in the claret shirts*) checking grapes on arrival at the winery.

the island; use of illegal labelling; use of unauthorised grape varieties; use of grapes with a potential alcohol below the legal minimum (9.0% abv).

In the unlikely event of breaches occurring, because the checks and visits described above prevent this, the main penalty is the imposition of fines depending on the type of offence and the severity. Other penalties could include the loss of products or business.

The directorate also disseminates information concerning EU aid and receives and controls applications for this aid. It will give advice to growers, producers and shippers, concerning the current wine regulations and will apply and enforce these.

Reception of grapes

During the harvest, two members of the Institute are present each day at the larger producers, to check the grapes when they arrive at the wineries. A 'mobile team' provides two people to supervise at the other producers when required. They monitor the quality of the grapes, confirm the variety, check weights and measure the potential alcohol.

The Institute can stop a producer accepting grapes if they do not reach the minimum quality, if they are not a recommended or authorised variety or if they are below the minimum potential alcohol.

During the control of the harvest, The Institute records the following information: date; producer code and place of receipt code; Institute team code; grower's identification number; number of plot; quantity (kg); potential alcohol. Any samples sent to the laboratory must be registered.

Harvest Book (Caderno de Vindima)

This document was issued to all growers for the first time, for the 2008 harvest. It records the grower's vineyard holdings and a section is completed each time the growers sell grapes to a producer. This enables The Institute to keep careful records of the harvest in terms of the weight of grapes, by variety, sold by each grower for the production of Madeira wine and table wines.

By 15th November following the harvest, the growers must declare their production for the year – 'Manifesto de Produção'. This is based on the Caderno de Vindima.

Final verification of harvest

In the final verification of the harvest, The Institute checks the quantities of wine produced and collects samples to send to the laboratory for quality control analysis.

Fortification

The producer must notify The Institute when purchasing alcohol for fortification. The alcohol must be tested and approved by The Institute before it can be used.

Sealing the *Estufas*

When producers decide to age their wines in an *Estufa*, they will contact the directorate. Seals will be placed on the *Estufa*, so that nothing can be added or removed. The seals will remain for at least 90 days. The temperature must not exceed 50°C. At the end of this time a member of the directorate will remove the seals.

When possible, The Institute carries out random inspections of *Estufas* to check temperatures and integrity of the seals.

REGIÃO AUTÓNOMA DA MADEIRA
INSTITUTO DO VINHO, DO BORDADO E DO ARTESANATO DA MADEIRA, I.P.

CADERNO 1 de 6

CADERNO DE VINDIMA 2008

Instituto Vinho, Bordado Artesanato Madeira, IP

Nº VITICULTOR: NIF:

MORADA:

CÓDIGO POSTAL:

FREGUESIA: Sé   CONCELHO: Funchal

LEFT Cover of Harvest Book, showing growers details.

Concentrated must

Any rectified concentrated grape must which is to be used for 'correcting' wines, must be tested and approved by The Institute before use.

Samples for analysis and tasting

Producers will complete a form when they wish samples to be collected for chemical analysis and tasting, prior to bottling.

Certificate of analysis and tasting

Before marketing, all wines must receive a seal of approval from The Institute. Samples will be collected and sent to the Quality Support Directorate laboratory for analysis. This can be carried out before or after bottling. It is usually carried out before bottling, because if the wine is bottled and then not approved, the bottles will have to be emptied and any necessary adjustments made to the wine, before submitting for a retest. The wines will also be subjected to a 'blind tasting' by an official tasting panel.

Results of the tests will be sent to the producer, and, if within the legal requirements will allow the wine to be bottled and sold. This particular certificate is only valid for 6 months. If some or all of the wine is not bottled within this period, the producer will have to resubmit samples for retesting before bottling.

ABOVE Samples to be sent to The Institute for testing.

IVBAM

If the wine does not reach the required standard, the producer can request a second test or alternatively can make adjustments to the wine before requesting a retest.

Seal of Guarantee (Selo de Garantia)

When the wine has reached the necessary standard, the producer will be able to purchase the necessary numbered seals of guarantee to place on the bottles. Seals can be purchased in advance and the details recorded in a 'current account'. After bottling, the labels and seals will be checked by The Institute.

Sales request and certificate

The producer must complete a form, 'request for certification of the Madeira wine' (RCVM) to sell wines to the Portuguese mainland, the Azores, EU countries and for export to other countries. This form will give the following data: customer; quantity; quality control information; labelling; number and size of bottles; the value of the wine.

If wines are to be exported, they will require a 'certificate of origin', issued by The Institute. A customs document (AAD), certified by The Institute, will also be required.

If wines are to be sold in the regional market the producer must complete a form, 'bottling Madeira wine for the regional market' and then a 'document of release for consumption' (DIC) will be issued (customs documents). Madeira wine is subject to excise duty (IEC).

Stocks of wine

The Institute keeps records of all wines produced and sold. A 'current account' is kept for each producer. A document, 'The Monthly Report', is completed by producers, giving details of all wine 'movements' for the previous month.

All of the above information enables The Institute to control the grapes from the time they arrive at the producers until they are bottled and sold/exported.

EU aid for producers

There are three types of EU aid available to producers:

Wine processing aid is available to producers for the production of Madeira wine and table wine ('DOP Madeirense' or 'IGP Terras Madeirenses').

Applications must be made to The Institute between 15th and 31st January, following the harvest. Currently, the value of the aid is €50 per tonne of grapes processed. **Wine aging aid** is available to producers who age Madeira wine for a period of five consecutive years. The wine can be aged in wooden casks or stainless steel containers of varying sizes. The Institute will seal and unseal the container at the beginning and end of the five-year period. Applications must be made to The Institute between 15th and 31st January, following the harvest. Currently, the value of the aid is €0.05 per hectolitre of wine per day of aging.

During the five-year period, producers may carry out processes to maintain the quality of the wine but the processes must not change the quantity. The Institute will remove the seal, supervise the process and reseal the container.

Madeira wine marketing aid is available to producers who sell their wines outside the island but within the EU market. Currently, the value of the aid is 10% of the value of the wine plus 10% of transport costs to the first port or airport of the country of destination.

Producers must submit details to The Institute, of labels they wish to use. The directorate will check these, to ensure they meet the standards of the country of destination. The Institute will check samples of bottles and labels after bottling and before sales. The label will need to include:

Brand

Protected designation of origin – 'Madeira' or 'Vinho da Madeira'

'Wine'

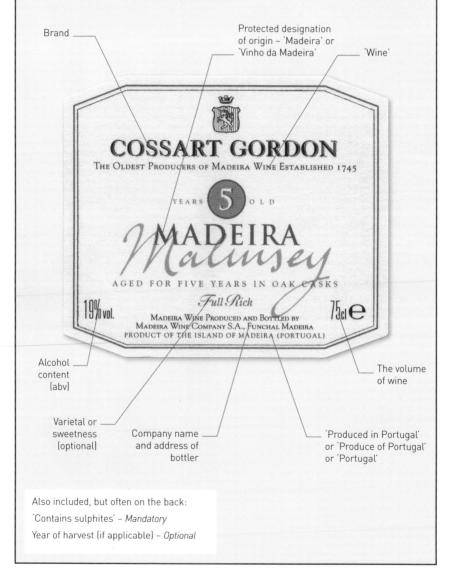

Alcohol content (abv)

The volume of wine

Varietal or sweetness (optional)

Company name and address of bottler

'Produced in Portugal' or 'Produce of Portugal' or 'Portugal'

Also included, but often on the back:
'Contains sulphites' – *Mandatory*
Year of harvest (if applicable) – *Optional*

The Quality Support Directorate

This directorate is responsible for ensuring wine quality, and has a laboratory for analysing wine samples. It also arranges for the wines to be tasted by a tasting panel.

The laboratory

All work must be carried out in accordance with European standards.

Six people work in the laboratory. When samples are submitted by producers, for official certification, the following analyses are carried out:

% alcohol abv (ethanol) by distillation;

volatile acidity by distillation and titration with standard sodium hydroxide (NaOH) solution;

EXAMPLE OF ANALYSIS RESULTS		
Parameter	Result	Units
Density at 20°C	1.0015	g/ml
Total alcohol (abv)	20.00	%vol
Baumé at 20°C	1.7	
Total dry extract	72.2	g/L
Total acidity	6.2	g/L tartaric acid
Volatile acidity	0.94	g/L acetic acid
Fixed acidity	5.0	g/L tartaric acid
pH	3.44	
3.5 diglucoside of malvidina	3	mg/L

*details of the relevant regulation would be given.

NB. Some countries will require analysis for other substances for Madeira wine eg. methanol, chlorides and sulphates.

APPROVAL PARAMETERS

Alcohol	17 % abv–22% abv

Style of Wine	Baumé
Dry	<1.5
Medium dry	1.0–2.5
Medium sweet	2.5–3.5
Sweet	> 3.5

Volatile acidity	
Current, 5 year	≤1.2g/L
≥10 years	≤1.5 g/L

3.5 diglucoside of malvidina	Max 15mg/L

ABOVE Testing samples in The Institute laboratory.

total acidity by titration with
standard sodium hydroxide
(NaOH) solution;
pH using a pH meter;
residual sugar using the Fehling's
test and measured in Baumé units;
density;
total dry extract;
3.5 – glucosido of Malvadina. This is
a test to show if any hybrid grapes
have been used in the wine. It is
carried out using fluorescence
spectrophotometry.

ABOVE Tasting samples in The Institute
tasting room.

The tasting panel

The panel consists of a minimum of
three and a maximum of five members.
They will mostly be from The Institute,
but also from the producers. All will be
experienced tasters and will undergo
a training programme.

FINAL % FOR EACH CATEGORY		
Appearance	Limpidity	16.0%
	Tonality	10.0%
Nose	Typicity	16.0%
	Intensity	10.0%
	Quality	12.0%
Taste	Attack	12.0%
	Evolution	12.0%
	Retronasal	12.0%
Total		100.0%

The scores from all of the tasters on the panel are
added and the average calculated for each category.
The average scores for each category are added to
give a total. To be approved, a wine must receive a
total score of 50% or more.

The wines will be tasted blind and
the only information given to the
tasters will be the age of the wine and
the style of sweetness. They will be
tasted in order of age, youngest first
and in order of style, dry, medium
dry, medium sweet and sweet.

The tasters will award marks for each
of 8 categories. Each category will be
assessed as:

Very Good; Good; Medium;
Mediocre, and marked accordingly
(see Tasting Sheet overleaf).

Approval

The analysis and tasting results will be
sent from the laboratory to the Wine
Sector and Regulation Directorate and
they will send them to the producer.

INSTITUTO DO VINHO, DO BORDADO E DO ARTESANATO DA MADEIRA,I.P.
Direcção de Serviços de Apoio à Qualidade - Câmara de Provadores

FICHA DE PROVAS - Denominação de Origem VLQPRD e VQPRD Madeirense

Data: 2009-01-22	Local da Prova CPROV- IVBAM		Temperatura °C		Sessão nº: 2009 / 8
		Vinho	Ambiente		

| Nº | Classe | Tipo | Fase visual | | | Fase olfactiva | | Fase gustativa | | | Notação | APRECIAÇÃO | | Obs. |
			Limpidez	Tonalidade	Tipicidade	Intensidade	Qualidade	Ataque	Evolução	Retronasal		Aprov.	Rep.	
1	Corrente	M/S	9	9	6,7	6,7	6,5	6,7	6,7	6,7	57,0	X		
2	Corrente	M/D	9	9	6,7	6,5	6,5		6,5	6,5	57,0	X		
3	Corrente	M/D	6,5	6,5	6,7	6,5	6,5	6,7	6,7	6,7	52,0	X		
4	Corrente	D	9	6,5	6,5	6,5	6,5	6,5	6,5	6,5	55,0	X		
5	5 Anos	M/S	9	9	6,5	6,5	6,5	6,5	6,5	6,5	57,0	X		
6	5 Anos	M/D	9	6,7	6,7	6,5	6,5	6,5	6,5	6,5	55,0	X		
7	10 Anos	M/S	9	9	6,5	9	9	9	6,5	6,5	64,0	X		
8	10 Anos	M/D	9	9	6,5	9	9	9	9	6,7	66,5	X		

O Provador: _____

	Pontuação sobre 100				
12,5 - Excelente	9,0 - Muito Bom	6,5 - Bom	3,0 - Medíocre	0 - Mau/Defeituoso	

Pág. 1/1

4ª Edição 2008/06/03

ABOVE An example of a completed tasting sheet for wines seeking Institute approval.

INSTITUE ANALYSIS OF SAMPLES

Year	Total Samples Analysed	Madeira Wine Samples Analysed	Disputed Results
2006	1817	979	0
2007	2112	988	0
2008	2305	1053	1

If the wine is not approved, the producer may request a retest. The second test cannot be disputed. Alternatively, the producer can make adjustments to the wine and then resubmit it for testing. It is more likely the producer will make 'corrections' rather than request a retest. Statistics from the Quality Support Directorate show only one disputed test in the past three years.

Other laboratory work

In addition to testing wines for certification, the laboratory participates in studies of the characteristics of Madeira wines and inter-laboratory work for the accreditation of equipment and methods of analysis.

Plans have been approved for the provision of a new laboratory for The Institute. It is anticipated this will be completed within the next two years.

Vitiviniculture Directorate

The directorate has a staff consisting of a Service Director, four office employees and five labourers. For viticultural work there is a Manager of Viticultural and Technical Coordination, a graduate responsible for coordination of the nursery vines and technical support, three technicians to give technical support to growers and to carry out work related to replanting inspections and licences, and viticultural projects, and for vine grafting. There are also 23 rural workers. All are full time.

For vitiviniculture, there are two graduates, a technician, two auxiliaries and an office employee.

Supervision of vine growing

There are approximately 1600 registered growers. Having only a small number of staff, it is not possible to regularly visit each of the growers. However, a technician from the directorate will visit to offer help and advice when requested by a grower. The main advice available involves the technical operations such as grafting, and pruning.

Soil samples can be collected and analysed and technical advice given. Often, due to their volcanic origin, soils have a high acidity, which can prevent the vines absorbing necessary elements such as magnesium. The acidity can be reduced by the addition of limestone-based products. Growers are eligible to receive 50% of the costs of these treatments. The acidity is measured in pH units on a scale 0–14. pH = 7 is neutral, pH below 7 is acid and above 7 is alkaline. The ideal level for vines is pH 6.5–7.0.

Meetings for growers are also arranged. These mainly take place between March and August and deal with various seasonal activities. Topics include pruning, treatment of pests and diseases, canopy management and general vine growing techniques. They also cover regulatory matters and aid to growers. These meetings are normally attended by up to 30 growers. Informational leaflets are distributed at the meetings.

Plantings and licences

The directorate issues licences for new plantings. A licence is required to plant more than 50 vines.

It is only possible to buy a plot of land, plant vines and sell the grapes for the production of Madeira wine or table wine, if the grower has acquired (eg bought) plantation rights, with or without the relocation of vines.

The EU regulations prohibit the increase in the total area of vines, but allows the Region (Madeira) to renovate the vines by authorising new plantations, if licensed by The Institute.

Although no new vineyard areas may be planted, The Institute can grant permission for replacement of vines in existing vineyards. This is carried out either by replacing existing *Vitis vinifera* vines (restructuring) or replacing American vines with *Vitis vinifera* (reconversion).

Grants are available covering 50% of investment, up to a maximum payment of €56,575.79. This does not cover irrigation, for which there is a separate programme.

During the time the vines are too young to produce grapes for wine, there is a compensation scheme of €3046 per hectare.

There has been a good response to support programmes for reconstruction and reconversion of vineyard areas during the past 8 years, with 274 projects involving a total of 86.80ha. It is predicted that during the support programme for a further four

REPLANTING PROJECTS		
	Nº Projects	Area (ha)
2001/2005	121	33.1161
2005/2006	26	10.0560
2006/2007	15	11.0305
2007/2008	74	23.3836
2008/2009	38	9.2200
Total	274	86.8062

years, until 2012–13, there will be a restructuring and reconversion of approximately 100ha.

When a request for replanting is made to The Institute, an inspection of the land will be carried out, and if considered suitable, a licence will be granted. Licences are issued subject to conditions that must be followed: the grape variety, the method of training, and the planting density.

VITIS VINIFERA PLANTINGS (HA) 2010					
CONCELHO (Council)	Complexa	Boal	Sercial	Tinta Negra	
Calheta	2.649	8.768	0.076	0.190	
Câmara de Lobos	2.324	6.601	8.644	161.027	
Funchal	1.304	0.219	0.107	0.125	
Machico	0.857	0.000	0.000	0.000	
Ponta do Sol	0.040	0.200	0.000	0.260	
Porto Moniz	1.346	0.000	6.415	0.040	
Porto Santo	0.000	0.000	0.000	0.000	
Ribeira Brava	0.414	3.696	0.287	5.443	
Santa Cruz	0.779	0.293	0.000	0.117	
Santana	17.237	0.070	0.785	0.134	
São Vicente	6.415	0.040	2.088	109.857	
TOTAL AREA (ha)	33.364	19.886	18.401	277.192	

Instituto do Vinho, do Bordado e do Artesanato da Madeira, IP

For *Espaldeira* the distance between vines is 1.4m and between rows 1.8m. For *Latadas* it is 2.0m between vines and between rows. The height of the *Latada* is not specified.

The *Espaldeira* system has several advantages over the *Latada*. The vines are less prone to diseases, and easier to treat when diseases are present. The quality of grapes is better although the yields are lower. However, it may not be possible to plant in the *Espaldeira* system because of the terrain. Currently, approximately 80% of plantings are on *Latadas* and 20% *Espaldeira*. There is a very small amount of bush vine plantings.

Growers selling grapes to producers of Madeira wine or table wine can also apply for a grant, the amount of which depends on the grape variety. Currently it is €500 per tonne for Verdelho, Sercial, Terrantez, Malvasia, Bastardo, Caracol and Listrão and €81 per tonne for other recommended and authorised varieties.

Register of vines

The Institute is in the process of producing a register of all vineyards. This is a monumental task, because there are so many tiny vineyard plots.

Currently, the approximate total plantings of *Vitis vinifera* vines for Madeira wines (fortified and table) is 493.7ha. Of this, approximately 58% is Tinta Negra; Sercial, Verdelho, Boal and Malvasia make up a further 23%, with the remainder being other approved or authorised varieties. The two largest areas of plantings are Câmara de Lobos and São Vincente.

Verdelho	Malvasia	Other White varieties	Other Red varieties	Total Area (ha)
5.369	0.208	0.457	1.118	18.861
7.745	0.760	0.590	0.190	187.880
0.417	0.459	0.112	0.150	2.892
0.419	0.320	0.342	7.809	9.819
0.150	0.000	0.100	0.040	0.790
9.881	0.375	1.600	16.093	35.751
0.300	0.000	11.462	0.000	11.762
0.485	0.750	0.000	0.280	11.354
0.030	0.000	0.000	0.740	1.959
6.272	35.021	7.269	3.550	70.337
16.010	0.813	5.181	1.913	142.318
47.177	**38.705**	**27.113**	**31.883**	**493.722**

ABOVE Verdelho clones. Part of The Institute's research project.

PREVIOUS PAGE Working in The Institute vineyards in Calheta.

Institute vineyards

The Institute has four vineyards, totalling approximately 3.7ha, in Estreito da Calheta, São Vincente, Câmara de Lobos and Arco de São Jorge. The largest, in Estreito da Calheta, is 1.8ha and is rented from the owners of the property. At the present time, these vineyards produce the mother vines to supply plants to The Institute's nursery in Caniçal.

This nursery area has three plots of approximately 0.5ha each. There is a grafting centre producing approximately 30,000 standard regional variety certified vines for sale to growers. This means that all new plantings for Madeira wine will come from the nursery. The main varieties grown are Sercial, Verdelho, Boal, Malvasia Cândida, Malvasia Roxa, Terrantez, Bastardo, Tinta Negra and Complexa.

The Institute does not grow vines for table wines but does grow some vines for table grapes.

Research

The Directorate is involved in a number of experimental projects:

- comparing grapes grown by the *Espaldeira* and *Latada* methods;
- comparing grapes grown by different pruning methods eg. Boal with Guyot and with Cordon. (There are no regulations about pruning methods).
- growing some Alicante Bouchet and Syrah vines;
- growing different rootstocks;
- growing different clones. At present they have five Sercial, five Verdelho, three Boal, three Malmsey and four Terrantez clones. It is hoped that they will be able to start selling these clones within the next 5–10 years.

Winemaking

The directorate does not have a responsibility to supervise wineries on the island. It is responsible for one winery, the Adega São Vincente, which belongs to the regional government. It is here that most of the island's table wines are made (*see* Chapter 11).

The Institute does make some Madeira wine. It is not sold, but used for Institute and Tourism Department functions. In 2008, 2000 litres were produced.

Promotional Services Department

The Department has 14 full time members, including two from the museum, one from the library and one from the handicrafts section.

It is responsible for promoting Madeira wines within the island and the rest of the world.

Regional promotions (including tourism)

Regional marketing on the island has two main targets: local consumers and tourists. The main goal is to increase knowledge about Madeira wines and their different styles, as well as introducing new ways of enjoying the wines which may attract new consumers.

Campaigns in the media, on the internet and outdoors, are held throughout the year. In addition, there are tastings, exhibitions and workshops. There is a newsletter, produced twice a year, providing information about all aspects of Madeira wine from viticulture to winemaking and consumption.

Each year there are three main regular campaigns, towards which many of the promotional strategies converge:

The Flower Festival This involves providing free tastings for tourists arriving at Madeira airport and on cruise liners. The festival is reinforced by outdoor and media campaigns.

Madeira on Ice This campaign takes place during the summer and is based in bars and restaurants where tastings are arranged to promote a new way of drinking Madeira wines – especially sweet Madeiras – with lemon and ice. Media campaigns are also held during this period.

Christmas and The New Year
Christmas time in Madeira is the traditional season for drinking Madeira wine. It is also the high season for visitors to the island, making it an excellent time of the year to strengthen all the wine campaigns and promotions.

ABOVE The Institute stand at the London International Wine Fair, 2010.

Mainland Portugal
The Madeira wine sector is represented at Wine Fairs that are held for professionals and consumers. The two main Fairs are held in Lisbon and Porto.

International promotions
The Institute is involved in promoting Madeira wine at the following annual Trade Fairs:

London International Wine Fair (LIWF)

Prowein, Dusseldorf.

A regular presence is also maintained by the Madeira wine sector at Vinexpo Bordeaux and Foodex Tokyo.

The Institute provides some financial help for producers to attend these events.

Trade tastings

The Institute, together with the producers, organizes annual tastings in the UK, France and Germany. There have also been tastings in the Czech Republic, Austria and Poland.

Recently, promotions have taken place in Japan, Brazil, Canada and the USA.

Other promotions

The Institute produces promotional literature and has recently produced a DVD (May 2009) and created a new website *www.vinhomadeira.pt.*

The Madeira Wine Association "Confraria"

The Madeira Wine Association was founded in 1985 and has its headquarters at The Institute. Its purpose is "to promote the good reputation of Madeira Wine all over the world".

The Association is comprised of:
The Chancellery, which administers and governs the Association;
The Table of Inspectors, which is the Fiscal Council of the Association;
The Chapter, which is the General Assembly of the Association.

The High Chancellor, a title of honour of the greatest prestige, presides over the Chapter and welcomes new members according to the traditions and rules of the Association. Whenever members meet officially, a Chapter takes place.

The Association's costume is made up of:
A long velvet cape, the colour of dark wine, reminiscent of the ruby Malmsey originating in Greece;
A black velvet hat with ostrich feathers in several colours, reminiscent of the 'gentlemen' and wealthy merchants of the first century of Madeira's colonisation, "who contributed much to the economic development of the island, planting vines that they used to bring in from distant lands";

The Tambuladeira, a small short cup, normally made of tin, with which new members are toasted. The bottom of the cup allows the light to reflect through the fine layer of wine, "so that its state of cleanliness and the colour of the precious liquid may be visible".

153

IVBAM

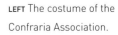

LEFT The costume of the Confraria Association.

Unfortified wines

The name 'Madeira', when used in the wine context, refers to the fortified wines of the island. However, unfortified wine is also made, which is called 'Table Wine'. There are two legal categories of 'Table Wine': classified by the EU as DOP (Protected Denomination of Origin) Madeirense and IGP (Protected Geographical Indication) Terras Madeirenses. The use of the term 'Table Wine' in these two different contexts can give rise to confusion, so I use the term 'Table Wines' to refer to the unfortified wines of the island.

There are currently 12 table wine producers on the island producing labelled wines. Justino's and MWC, are the only fortified Madeira wine producers that also make table wines. The wine of the other ten producers

ABOVE Preparing the winery for the next harvest.

is made at The Institute's winery, the Adega São Vicente. At the present time, it would not be viable for others to build and maintain a winery.

The winery was opened in1999 and extended in 2005. It has a capacity of 300,000 litres, with temperature control. Well equipped, it has a range of stainless steel tanks for fermentation and storage, from 200 litres – 15,500 litres, two pneumatic presses with capacities of 2.5 tonnes and 9.0 tonnes, storage for barrels which are owned by the producers, a bottling line which averages 800–1000 bottles per hour, and a laboratory.

It has six full time staff, with an additional five or six during the harvest, to enable work to be carried out in two shifts.

There are two forms of contract by which the wines can be made:

1. The winery is responsible for the complete production process. Grapes are received from the producer on an agreed date and, after consultation, the resident winemaker will make the wines.

2. The producer may use their own winemaker at The Institute's facilities.

Currently 8 of the 10 producers using the facilities, have their wines made by the Institute's winemaker, one has a winemaker who uses the facilities and one has a 'joint' contract, where some wine is made by The Institute's winemaker and the rest by the producer's winemaker. The minimum quantity of grapes accepted from a producer is 2.5 tonnes for white grapes and 3.5 tonnes for reds. Anything less would not be economic.

The winery also provides a bottling service for producers who make their own wine. Such wines will be analysed and must meet all legal requirements before bottling.

In 2009 the total table wine produced was 148,315 litres.

Grape varieties

A large number of grapes can be used.

DOP Madeirense

White grapes Verdelho, Terrantez, Malvasia Cândida, Boal (Malvasia Fina), Sercial, Alvarinho Lilaz, Rio Grande, Carão de Moça, Arnsburger, Sauvignon Blanc, Chardonnay, Ugni Blanc, Chenin Blanc, Malvasia Bianca, Malvasia Cândida Branca; Malvasia de São Jorge.

Red grapes Tinta Negra, Malvasia Roxa (for rosé wines), Bastardo, Deliciosa, Touriga Nacional, Tinta Barroca, Maria Feld, Merlot, Cabernet Sauvignon, Complexa, Touriga Franca, Shiraz, Aragonez.

IGP Terras Madeirenses

White grapes Arinto, Arnsburger, Boal, Carão de Moça, Chardonnay, Chenin Blanc, Malvasia Cândida, Malvasia de São Jorge, Sauvignon Blanc, Sercial, Terrantez, Ugni Blanc, Verdelho.

Red grapes Aragonez, Bastardo, Cabernet Sauvignon, Complexa, Deliciosa, Malvasia Roxa (for rosé wines), Merlot, Tinta Barroca, Tinta Negra Mole, Touriga Franca, Touriga Nacional, Shiraz.

LEFT Obtaining a tank sample for tasting and analysis.

Winemaking

When grapes arrive at the winery in the minimum accepted quantities they are checked for quality (clean, disease free) and the pH and potential alcohol are measured. The minimum acceptable potential alcohol is 10% although 10.5% is normally required.

The winemaker will discuss and offer advice to the producer/owner, concerning the style of wine required. As a result, a range of techniques is employed at the winery. These may include:

skin contact (10–16 hours) for some Verdelho wines;

pumping over for red wines;

some carbonic maceration;

some barrel fermentation, currently for two wines, a 100% Verdelho, and a wine with three varieties, (Arnsberger, with some Verdelho, and Boal);

use of a range of cultured yeasts.

Fermentation

White wines are fermented between 14–16°C, and red wines > 25°C.

Red wines undergo malolactic fermentation. Sometimes this occurs naturally, but in most cases specific malolactic bacteria are used because of the low temperatures post harvest/ post alcoholic fermentation.

Oak

Oak chips, staves and French and American barrels are used.

Stabilisation

Cold stabilisation is not used to remove tartrates from white wines. Instead, metatartaric acid is added. This is an effective way of preventing precipitation of tartrates but is only effective for a limited time. The wines should be drunk within two years.

Preventing oxidation

If the fermentation and storage tanks are not full, they are topped with argon or nitrogen gas to prevent oxidation.

Bottling

Before bottling, wines are analysed in the laboratory. The checks include: alcohol; residual sugar; pH, free and total sulphur dioxide and volatile acidity. All wines must be analysed at The Institute's laboratory. Only new bottles are used. They are washed with a solution containing tartaric acid and potassium metabisulphite solution (1%) before use.

Alcohol

For DOP Madeirense wines the minimum alcohol content is 10.5% abv for white and rosé wines, and 11.5% abv for red wines.

For IGP Terras Madeirenses wines the minimum alcohol content is 10.0% abv for white and rosé wines, and 10.0% for red wines.

The wines

It is really too early to make a judgement on Madeiran table wines. As can be seen in the tables above, producers can use a wide range of red and white grapes.

PRODUCTION		
The chart shows the production of table wine for the past five years		
Year	DOP Madeirense (litres)	IGP Terras Madeirenses (litres)
2005	163,817	65,415
2006	139,990	46,374
2007	76,882	29,145
2008	107,670	24,041
2009	125,994	22,321

ABOVE Cleaning casks (*barriques*).

Arnsburger is used in many white wines, but unfortunately has a neutral taste. It is interesting to note that The Institute is not, for the time being, allowing any new plantings of this grape. Good quality white wines can be made from Verdelho.

It may be that good quality red wines will be made from Touriga Nacional, Tinta Roriz and a few other red grapes. Time will tell.

A problem for the development of table wines is the cost. Everything except the grapes must be imported, thus involving high costs and putting high prices on the finished wines. The wines are sold in wine shops, supermarkets and restaurants but not, so far, exported.

TABLE WINES AVAILABLE IN 2010				
Name of wine/brand	Producer	Classification DOP or IGP	Grapes used with%	Comments about Winemaking
Atlantis Rosé	MWC	DOP Madeirense	Tinta Negra	Wine made at MWC
Barbusano Verdelho	Quinta do Barbusano Lda	DOP Madeirense	Verdelho	No oak
Columbo Tinto	Justinos	IGP Terras Madeirenses	Touriga Nacional (40%), Complexa, Tintas Negra	Wine made at Justino's
Columbo Branco	Justinos	IGP Terras Madeirenses	Arnsburger	Wine made at Justino's
Euxurros Tinto	Ricardo França Soc Unipessoal Lda	DOP Madeirense	Tinta Negra, Complexa, Merlot Cab Sauvignon	
Euxurros Branco	Ricardo França Soc Unipessoal Lda	DOP Madeirense	Verdelho Arnsburger	
Palmeira e Voltas	Octávio Ascensão Ferraz	DOP Madeirense	Verdelho Boal Arnsburger	
Quinta do Moledo Tinto Reserva	João Mendes Soc Unipessoal Lda	DOP Cab Madeirense	Sauvignon, Merlot	
Quinta do Moledo Verdelho Reserva	Ricardo França Soc Unipessoal Lda	DOP Madeirense	Verdelho	Oak
Rocha Tinto	Ricardo França Soc Unipessoal Lda	DOP Cab Madeirense	Sauvignon, Complexa	
Rocha Branco	Ricardo França Soc Unipessoal Lda	DOP Madeirense	Arnsburger	
Seiçal Tinto 2007	Seiçal – Soc De Prod de Vinho do Seixal, Lda	DOP Madeirense	Cab Sauvignon Merlot, Tinta Roriz, Touriga Nacional	Staves
Seiçal Tinto Reserva 2007	Seiçal – Soc De Prod de Vinho do Seixal, Lda	DOP Madeirense	Touriga Nacional Cabernet Sauvignon	Oak Barrels

TABLE WINES AVAILABLE IN 2010

Name of wine/brand	Producer	Classification DOP or IGP	Grapes used with%	Comments about Winemaking
Terras do Avô Branco	Duarte Caldeira & Filhos, Seixal Wines Lda	DOP Madeirense	Verdelho (95%) Arnsburger (5%)	1st vintage 2008
Torcaz Tinto	Francisco Alberquerque	DOP Madeirense	T N (75%) Merlot (25%)	
Torcaz Branco	Ricardo França Soc Unipessoal Lda	DOP Madeirense	Verdelho	
Vinha da Palmeira Branco	Octávio Ascensão Ferraz	DOP Madeirense	Verdelho, Boal, Arnsburger	6months in new French oak
Pedra de Fogo	Elsa Maria Ferreira	DOP Madeirense	Touriga Nacional Cab Sauvignon	Staves
Cabeço da Queimada	Luís Ferreira	IGP Terras Madeirenses	Touriga Nacional, Cab Sauvignon; Tinta Barroca	Staves
Ponta do Tristão Branco 2007	Qta do Barbusano Lda	DOP Madeirense	66,6 Arnsburger; 33,4 Verdelho	
Xavelha Tinto 2007	Octávio Ascensão Ferraz	IGP Terras Madeirenses	Cab Sauvignon, Complexa	
Palheiros Tinto 2007	Seiçal – Soc de Prod de Vinho do Seixal, Lda	IGP Terras Madeirenses	Cab Sauvignon, Merlot, Touriga Nacional, Tinta Barroca	Oak Chips
Seiçal Rosé 2007	Seiçal – Soc de Prod de Vinho do Seixal, Lda	DOP Madeirense	Cab Sauvignon, Merlot, Touriga Nacional, Tinta, Barroca Complexa, Tinta Roriz, Shiraz	
Barbusano Rosé – Touriga Nacional	Qta do Barbusano Lda	DOP Madeirense		

Chapter 12
The Future

Looking ahead

As we have seen, the number of producers of Madeira wine has contracted considerably in the last 100 years, to just eight today. The days when Madeira commonly graced the decanters and dining tables of the wealthy are gone – today they are more likely to have Bordeaux wines that are highly rated by Robert Parker, to show to their dining companions. Fortified wines generally have been in decline. Sherry has suffered particularly, and great Port wines are sold for relatively low prices. The lost markets may well never reappear, and Madeira must work to find new, young customers wherever they may be in the world, as well as suggesting different and innovative ways and moments to taste one of the most famous and oldest wines in the world.

Since 1986, when Portugal joined the EU, considerable investments have been made in the Madeira wine industry. At the present time, funds are still available to growers and producers in the form of grants. In this chapter I will look at the challenges facing the industry and the measures that are being taken and others that might be taken, to overcome problems and lead to further development and progress. Clearly, there are many factors that will determine the future of the Madeira wine industry.

Viticulture

The growers

The world recession has obviously had an adverse affect on the sales of fortified Madeira wines. As previously described in Chapter 9, the amount of grapes purchased by the companies is based on sales and stocks of wines. For the 2009 harvest, this could have meant growers would not be able to sell all their grapes. However, financial incentives were introduced by the government to help producers purchase more grapes than the minimum required by current regulations. The amount of grapes purchased by each producer is, of course, limited by their winemaking capacity as well as their success in the market.

One important reason for the introduction of financial incentives is in recognition of the work carried out by the companies. They have, in recent years, made considerable efforts in modernisation and marketing. This has helped to consolidate the quality and the image of Madeira wines and to recover sales. It has meant that the producers have had to take on considerable financial responsibilities, consequently reducing their capacity to deal with harvest campaigns in terms of buying sufficient grapes to satisfy their normal business expectations.

Unfortunately, the 2009 harvest was affected by wet weather earlier in the year, which meant some growers experienced difficulty in achieving the desired degree of ripeness in their grapes. Official figures from The Institute show that a total of 3.9 million kg were used to make Madeira wine in 2009, which is a reduction of 16.4% compared with 2008. Government help was made available to growers whose grapes did not ripen sufficiently for them to be sold for the production of Madeira wine. Such financial help as described above, can only be made available in exceptional circumstances.

Viticulture on the island is very difficult. Vines are often grown in tiny plots mainly on steep slopes and using the *Latada* system. This means working in the vineyards is very hard and labour intensive. Even in the 10ha Quinta Grande vineyard of Henriques & Henriques, picking has to be done by hand. It is hard to see how any form of mechanisation could ever be used. Working in the vineyards is not something that attracts many young people. However, it would seem that in recent years more of the younger members of growers' families have become interested and involved. It is essential for the future of the industry that this trend continues.

Improving grape quality

It is well known that high quality grapes are needed to make high quality wines. What is to prevent some growers just doing the minimum necessary to reach the basic ripeness and hygiene necessary to sell their crop? The price paid per kg by producers depends on the health of the grapes and the level of potential alcohol above the minimum required (9.0% abv). Any measures to improve the quality of grapes will mean persuading some growers to change some of the practices that have grown up over centuries. Sceptical growers need to be given assurances that any changes, although initially costly, will be of benefit to them in the long term.

Yields are currently restricted to 80hL/ha but, in certain years, this can be increased in consultation with The Institute. This happened in 2008 and 2009 when the yield allowed was 150hL/ha. Many would question whether high quality fruit can come from such a high yield. However, the natural conditions of the region, with its very rich soils and favourable climate, together with ongoing improvements in viticultural techniques, may, in the near future, provide a more adequate yield, truly reflecting the required quality, without the need for concessions.

Many growers have been persuaded to take measures to improve the quality of their grapes and some have even ventured into organic production. Maybe more will follow? In 2008 Justino's purchased 15,000kg of organically certified Tinta Negra grapes. These have been used to produce a sweet Madeira wine which the company hopes to bottle in 10 or 15 years time.

Increasing plantings

Clearly, there is a need to plant more of the recommended vine varieties for fortified Madeira wine, especially the white varieties of which approximate current plantings (2009) are Sercial 15ha, Verdelho 36ha, Boal 21ha and Malvasias 32ha. There is a particular issue with Verdelho. The companies would like to buy more but there is also demand for this variety from the producers of table wine. According to Institute statistics, between 2004–9, the amount of Verdelho sold to the Madeira companies varied from a high of 43 tonnes in 2005 to a low

of 35 tonnes in 2009. However, the cultivation of Verdelho has increased over the past 10 years. In 1999 there were 27.79ha and in 2009 this had increased to 35.91ha. The Institute is working to promote the growing of more Verdelho.

It is disappointing that EU regulations do not permit further planting from the present time until 2015. Fortunately, there has been a good response to take part in programmes for replacing old *Vitis vinifera* vines with new vines (reconstruction) and replacing non *Vitis vinifera* vines with *vinfera* vines (reconversion). 77.6ha have been planted in the past 8 years and it is predicted that the support programme for 2008–9 to 2012–13, will involve approximately 100ha more.

Only *Vitis vinifera* grapes can be used to produce fortified Madeira wines or table wines. At the present time, Madeira has approximately 500ha of *Vitis vinifera* vines. There are still some areas planted with American vines, including Jacquet, Isabella and Cunningham, which are used by the growers to make wine, vinho seco, exclusively for personal consumption. This consumption is decreasing and The Institute is assisting in the progressive abandonment of these vines and the reconversion to new *Vitis vinifera* plantings.

Innovation

Reading about Madeira wines, one occasionally one sees reference to the increasingly 'rare' Terrantez, Bastardo and Moscatel grape varieties. It is therefore interesting to note an increase in the production of Terrantez grapes in the past few years. In 2009, 2206kg were used in the production of Madeira wine. I believe this is a variety from which extremely good wines can be produced. Hopefully this increase will continue and maybe more of all three of these varieties will be grown in future?

ABOVE Experimental Verdelho vines at Barbeito's winery.

At Barbeito, they have an experimental planting of a small number of vines. When asked about the planting, Ricardo de Freitas commented "We planted Verdelho to test the how the vineyards would react to our micro-climate. At this altitude only the Sercial seems to grow without problems. So we are just trying to learn some lessons for the future".

Experimental work is being carried out at The Institute's vineyards. These involve: comparing different training and pruning methods; growing different rootstocks; growing different clones. Since all future vines for the production of Madeira wines will come from The Institute nursery, it is to be hoped that this will result in improvements in quality.

Winemaking

There has been a considerable investment by producers both in new premises and in winery equipment, as detailed in Chapter 8. There is a strong commitment by all producers to improve the quality of wines produced by the *Estufa* process. In recent years, a reduction in the temperatures used has resulted in fresher wines with less burnt flavours.

Research

The Institute

As stated above, The Institute is involved in a number of experimental projects. The outcomes of these studies should help both growers and producers to continue to improve the quality of grapes and Madeira wines. One current project is to certify some Verdelho clones that the Viticultural Department of the Institute has obtained from clonal selection

LEFT Checking Malvasia vines at The Institute winery.

work since 1990. Once these clones are certified by the national authority, they will become the exclusive property of the Madeira region and will be reproduced under authorisation from the Madeiran authorities.

The University

In 1998, Professor J Marques at the University of Madeira, together with Dr Constantino, then President of the Madeira Wine Institute, commenced research into various aspects of the production of Madeira wines and their characteristics. So far, this has involved the study of aromas and grape varieties, the composition of wines, and the *Estufagem* process.

Aromas

These studies have looked at the many factors influencing aromas, including soil, climate, grape variety and production methods. The intention is to determine the typical composition and aromas of wines, both young and old, in order to help producers have a better control over the final bouquet of the variety and style of wine they wish to make.

Composition of wines

Wines are very complex, containing several hundreds of compounds, including organic acids, amino acids, aromas, sugars and polyphenols. Most are related to the fermentation and aging processes and have an important impact on the bouquet and also the stability and balance of the wine. These studies aim to determine how the various compounds evolve. The results could help producers to adjust fermentation and aging processes to improve the quality of their wines.

The *Estufagem* process

The main aromas of Madeira wines, 'dried fruits', 'toast' and 'candy' are related to the aging process. The composition changes, depending on the temperature, the length of aging and the sugar content. One of the main characteristics of aged Madeiras is the brown colour that results mainly from the degradation of sugars and is independent of grape variety. It is

LEFT Using a gas chromatograph to identify Madeira wine aromas.

known that other foodstuffs turn brown when heated.

Professor Marques is studying the compounds responsible for the colour. He is attempting to determine the main chemical reactions occurring during the oxidative aging process and provide information for producers about the colour and composition of wines. This should help them to control the *Estufagem* process to obtain the desired wine quality.

ABOVE Sampling wine from an experimental *Estufa* at the University.

POSEI

The POSEI scheme has encouraged producers to age wines for the five years required, but obviously producers do need an earlier return on some of their stocks and the 3-year-old (current) remains the most popular category. In 2009, this accounted for 63.3% of sales. One way to get added value has been the marketing of the superior produce of Single Casks – interesting small quantities of individual wines. The premium price achieved outweighs the high cost of working with such small quantities. The superior quality of these wines should help boost the image of Madeira generally. Such quality perceptions hopefully cascade down to the younger wines, just as in Bordeaux, where the classed growths impact on the image of the region's wines generally.

Colheita

The Colheita category – selling single harvest wines before the 20 years required to market them as Frasqueira (vintage) wines – is of growing importance. Perhaps the main challenge to this category is getting the consumer to understand the term and the tremendous value this category represents.

Blending grapes

Another innovation is the blending of two of the recommended white varieties, the wine produced is then marketed by the company under a brand. The MWC produces Blandy's 'Alvada'. This is a 5-year-old wine made from a blend of 50% each of Malmsey and Boal.

Barbeito makes 'VB' which is a blend of Verdelho and Boal.

Some people might argue that blending the varieties is a mistake, but results so far are certainly impressive and the wines are much sought after.

Single casks

Bottling from single casks is another innovation. When winemakers discover that a particular cask has developed 'special' characteristics, they will bottle the wine rather than keeping it to become part of a large blend. Ricardo Freitas at Barbeito is becoming well known for this. Recently he found two 'special' casks of Boal, casks 48 and 84, which he blended and bottled. This seems an enterprising way to market small lots (*lotes*) of wine. Like the wines made by blending two varieties, they are much sought after.

Marketing

If sales are to increase then there is a need to find new consumers, particularly young consumers. In order to do this, thought will need to be given to finding new ways for consumers to enjoy Madeira wines. Already, there is the summer 'with ice' promotion on the island. Maybe this should be extended to other markets.

LEFT Alvada wine produced by MWC.

Most people who have tasted or have heard of Madeira would probably not think of it as a 'food wine'. Producers do mention food and wine pairings (*see* Chapter 6). Maybe there is an opportunity here to promote the idea much more positively than at present. A medium sweet Boal or a sweet Malmsey Madeira is, I believe, an ideal wine to partner chocolate.

International

In a wine world that seems to be dominated by over-production on the one hand, and the power of the anti-alcohol lobby on the other, even maintaining existing markets is challenging for all wine producers, and the ability to break into new ones daunting. Producers have to be proactive, but also listen to market demands. At present two producers are not currently selling to the UK, but it is well known that supermarket dominance and the decline in high street multiple specialists in the UK has made breaking into the market extremely difficult. It is therefore pleasing to note in a press report (May 2010) "Waitrose reports that sales of Madeira have risen by 20%

over the last year and the supermarket now stocks 17 different brands compared to five just two years ago".

There has been an increase in the number of markets in recent years. In 2007, Madeira wines were sold to 14 new countries/markets. Whilst the sales of these 14 only accounted for approximately 4% of total sales in each of the last three years (2007–2009), this is clearly a great step forward. Also encouraging, is the establishment of four more new markets in 2009 – Australia, Dubai, Macau and Singapore.

Local

In 2009, local sales on the island accounted for approximately 14% of total sales. Wines from most of the producers are readily available in shops, supermarkets or directly from the producer. Official figures for 2008 show the population was 247,161 and that the island receives approximately 1 million tourists a year. While most tourists come by air and are therefore limited by the amount they can carry, visitors on cruise liners can carry more. There is potential here for increasing sales. Perhaps the key to

maximising the benefit from these visitors is to make them ambassadors for the wines of Madeira when they return home.

Tastings

It would seem vitally important to offer visitors the opportunity to taste wines. Most of the producers do have tasting rooms. However, unless they are proactive, with well advertised tastings which are easy to access, opportunities for sales may be lost.

Hotels often give a 'welcome party' for visitors, which includes a tasting of Madeira wines. A free small glass of 'Madeira' is often given at the end of meals in restaurants. If this is the first time the visitor has ever tasted Madeira wine, it is vitally important to ensure that the wine provided is of good quality. Should this first taste not prove to be a pleasurable experience, then it is unlikely the tourists will want to visit the producers to taste more, or buy wine to drink whilst on the island or to take home. I believe this offers a great opportunity for producers and hoteliers

LEFT Barbeito Boal blended from Casks 48 & 84.

to work together. This may seem an insignificant matter until one thinks of how many visitors the island receives in a year.

International investment

Two companies are owned or part owned by companies from other countries – Justino's (France) and Barbeito (Japan). Symingtons, Port producers in mainland Portugal, are the major shareholder in the MWC. When money is invested from outside the island, this has the potential to help to promote sales and open up markets.

Joint enterprise

Groups of wine producers from many countries and individual regions within them, work together to promote their wines. This has been very successful in the UK in recent years, particularly with wines from the 'new world' countries. A group of wine producers from the Douro region in Portugal has had similar success with their unfortified wines.

In today's difficult marketing conditions it is essential, in order to make the maximum impact, that exporters work together in this way. I believe this certainly applies to the seven Madeira producers who export their wines. The closer they can work together to promote the image of

Madeira wine throughout the world, the greater their success will be. Within the group, it is important that they promote not only Madeira wine, but also the range of individual company styles available. Already, as described Chapter 10, The Institute and the producers are involved in a number of promotions, tastings and sales visits worldwide. It is vital that they build on this because, with a strong spirit of cooperation, an extremely difficult task will be made easier.

Regulations

At the time of writing, meetings were taking place between the producers and The Institute to review existing regulations and, where necessary, make proposals for updating or revising, in order to make improvements for the island's wine industry.

I note that, at present, there is no requirement to state the date of bottling on labels for Colheita and Frasqueira (vintage) wines. Wines can change considerably with additional years in cask. This means, for example, a 1980 Frasqueira (vintage) wine bottled in 2005 will be very different from the same wine bottled in 2010. To make the date of bottling on labels mandatory would, I believe, be helpful in removing any possible confusion for the consumer.

Maybe the word 'vintage' could also be used, as it is for Port. Again, this would be helpful for consumers.

Most Madeira wines are made from Tinta Negra grapes. Despite this, the name of the grape is not currently permitted on the label. Maybe, particularly as the quality of wines has increased so much in recent years, the time has come to allow wines made from at least 85% Tinta Negra grapes, to indicate this on the label.

Table wines

Production of table wine on the island (*see* Chapter 11) has averaged approximately 160,000 litres over the past five years (2005–2009). This is very small compared with the average production of 4 million litres of fortified Madeira wine for the same period. It is perhaps surprising that only two Madeira producers are making and marketing table wines. In mainland Portugal, the Douro valley was always known for production of fortified wine – Port. However, during the last 20 years many exciting unfortifed wines have been made, both by the Port companies and individual, small wineries. These often sell for higher prices than achieved for Port, and their success has been beyond expectations. Unlike Madeira, they have many well established vineyards with a wide range of grape varieties.

Nevertheless, this may be one possible way forward for the island's wine industry. Table wines produced on the island could replace those currently imported from mainland Portugal, for sale to islanders and visitors, thus helping the island's economy.

Some final thoughts

The best Madeira wines are always going to command high prices. This, I believe, applies to all top quality wines. However, it is important that all wine lovers should be able to afford to experience the pleasures of Madeira. During my many visits to the island, I have been extremely impressed by the enthusiasm of producers and their teams for their wines. Given the huge amount of time and effort that goes into the production of these wines, they represent excellent value for money. This should, I believe, mean there will always be a place in the market for Madeira wines.

I further believe the quality of the wines will continue to improve as more high quality grapes become available. With skilful marketing campaigns, especially on the island, sales should increase. As more wine lovers around the world discover the excitement and pleasure of Madeira wines I hope that the 'golden age' of Madeira will emerge again in the not too distant future.

Additional information

Glossary

abv Alcohol by volume, expressed as a percentage.

Acids The main acid in unripe grapes is malic acid. As grapes ripen tartaric becomes the main acid. Together malic and tartaric acids constitute over 90% of acidity in grapes. Tartaric, malic, acetic, succinic, and many other acids are found in wines.

American rootstocks Rootstocks from American vine species, onto which are grafted European vinifera vines. The rootstocks are resistant to phylloxera.

American vines Vines of the genus Vitis (not vinifera), which originated in North America.

American hybrid vines Vines produced by crossing different American vine species or by crossing American species with European vinifera species.

Baumé A scale of measurement used to determine the sugar content of must.

Bentonite An aluminosilicate clay that has powerful adsorption properties, $Al_4Si_8O_{20}(OH)_4nH_2O$, used for clarifying wines.

Cadastro A record of vineyards showing areas and grape varieties.

Caderno A card, introduced in 2008, to record grapes sold by growers to producers.

Canteiro Wooden beams on which casks are placed during the aging of wines.

Concelho Local council.

Espaldeira Sytem of training vines in rows on wires between posts

Estufa Stainless steel or lined concrete tank in which the estufgem process takes place.

Estufagem Process of treating and aging wine by heating at 45–50°C for a minimum of 3 months.

Fructose A sugar occurring in grapes and other fruits, formula $C_6H_6O_6$.

Garrafeira A category of Madeira wine which has been cask aged for a minimum of twenty years (aka Frasqueira).

Glucose A sugar occurring in grapes and other fruits, formula $C_6H_6O_6$.

Hydrometer Glass bulb with a calibrated stem, used to measure density of liquids.

IVBAM Instituto do Vinho do Bordado e do Artesanato da Madeira, IP – Wine, Embroidery and Handicraft Institute of Madeira.

Kieselguhr A form of earth mined in Germany and consisting of skeletal remains of tiny sea creatures. In fine powder form, it is used in earth filters.

Latada Trellis for supporting vines.

Lote Specific parcel of wine (English – Lot)

Malmsey The name often used for sweet Madeira wines made from Malvasia grapes.

Malvina Substance (anthocyanin glucoside) found in American hybrid vines.

Mangra Madeiran word for powdery mildew.

Must Unfermented or partially fermented grape juice, with or without skins and other grape solids.

Potassium Metabisulphite $K_2S_2O_5$ A white powder which provides a source of sulphur dioxide.

pH A measure of the acidity of a solution. It is measured using a pH meter, which gives readings on a scale 0–14. The lower the reading, the higher the acidity. pH = 7 is neutral, ph>7 is alkaline.

Poios Terraces with retaining walls.

Precipitate A solid that is thrown out of solution.

Press juice Juice that is extracted from grapes by pressure.

Refractometer Instrument for measuring the density of grape juice. The readings give either the sugar content or the potential alchol (abv). Modern refractometers give a digital readout.

Solera A system of blending, where a small amount is drawn from a reserve for bottling and is replaced by a younger, similar wine. The younger wine is allowed to blend and mature with the remainder of the reserve. The process can be repeated annually, for up to 10 years.

Sulphur dioxide (SO_2) A compound used in winemaking to inhibit spoilage by oxidation and bacteria. Often added in the form of potassium metabisulphite.

Vinha da Roda Wine that was shipped on a round sea voyage (17th – 20th century) to improve the quality.

Vinho Seco Table wine made for local consumption, from American hybrid vines.

Useful contacts

ARTUR DE BARROS E SOUSA LDA
Rua dos Ferreiros 109
9000–082 Funchal
Tel: +351 291 220 622
e-mail: *absl@netmadeira.com*
www.vinhosmadeira.com

HM BORGES, SUCRS, LDA
Rua 31 de Janeiro, 83
9050–011 Funchal
Tel: +351 291 223 247
Fax: +351 291 222 281
e-mail: *info@hmborges.com*
www.hmborges.com

J FARIA & FILHOS, LDA
Travessa do Tanque, 85 e 87
9020–258 Funchal
Tel: +351 291 742 935
Fax: +351 291 742 255
e-mail: *jfariafilhos@sapo.pt*

UK Agent
Atlantico UK Ltd.,
Unit 10, Commerce Park,
Commerce Way,
Croydon CR0 4ZS
Tel:020 8649 7444
e-mail: *info@atlantico.co.uk*

HENRIQUES & HENRIQUES,
  VINHOS SA
Sitio de Belém
9300 Câmara de Lobos
Tel: +351 291 941 551
Fax: +351 291 941 590
e-mail:
  henriquesehenriques@netmadeira.com
www.henriquesehenriques.pt

UK Agent
Mentzendorff & Co Ltd
27–29, Albert Embankment
London SE1 7TJ
Tel: 020 7840 3600
Fax: 020 7840 3601
e-mail: *info@mentzendorff.co.uk*

JUSTINO'S, MADEIRA WINES, SA
Parque Industrial da Cancela
9125–042 Caniço
Santa Cruz
Tel: +351 291 934 257
Fax: +351 291 934 049
e-mail: *justinos@justinomadeira.com*
www.justinosmadeira.com

MADEIRA WINE COMPANY
Rua dos Ferreiros, 191
9000–082 Funchal
Tel: +351 291 740 100
Fax: +351 291 740 101
e-mail:
  semerces@madeirawinecompany.com
www.madeirawinecompany.com

UK Agent
John E Fells & Son,
Prince Edward House
Berkhamstead HP4 3EZ
Tel: 01442 870900
e-mail: *info@fells.co.uk*

**PEREIRA D'OLIVEIRA
(VINHOS), LDA**
Rua dos Ferreiros, 107
9000–082 Funchal
Tel: +351 291 220 784
Fax: +351 291 229 081
e-mail: *perolivinhos@hotmail.com*

UK Agent
Bovey Wines
12, Higher Tristram
Polzeath
Wadebridge
Cornwall PL27 6TF
Tel: 01208 862613
e-mail: *boveywines@btconnect.com*

**VINHOS BARBEITO
(MADEIRA), LDA**
Estrada da Ribeira Garcia
Parque Empresarial de Câmara
    de Lobos - Lote 8
9300–324 Câmara de Lobos
Tel: +351 291 761 829
Fax: +351291 765 832
e-mail: *info@barbeito.com.pt*
www.vinhosbarbeito.com

UK Agent
Raymond Reynolds Ltd.,
Furness Vale Industrial Estate
Station Road
High Peak
Derbyshire SK23 7SW
Tel: 01663 742230
e-mail: *info@raymondreynolds.co.uk*

**IVBAM – Instituto do Vinho, do Bordado
    e do Artesanato da Madeira, IP**
Rua Visconde de Anadia, 44
9050–020 Funchal
Tel: +351 291211615
e-mail: *ivbam.sra@gov-madeira.pt*
www.vinhomadeira.pt

**Secretaria Regional do Turismo
    e Transportes**
Tel: +351 291 211 900
Fax: +351 291 232 151
e-mail: *info.srtt@gov-madeira.pt*
*www.madeiraislands.travel/pls/madeira/
    wsmwhom0.home*

Aeroporto da Madeira
Tel: +351 291 520 700
e-mail: *anam@anam.pt*
www.anam.pt/Default.aspx

**Hospital Central do Funchal – Dr. Nélio
    Mendonça**
Tel: +351 291 705 666
    and +351 291 705 641
e-mail: *sec.geral@srs.pt*

Production and Sales 2008-2009

VITIS VINIFERA PRODUCTION 2009 (KG)

Council	Growers	Aragones	Arnsburger	Cabernet Sauvignon	Merlot	Syrah	Tinta Barroca	Touriga Franca	
Calheta	73	0	0	2,957	797	18	0	0	
Câmara de Lobos	721	0	463	43	305	0	25	0	
Funchal	94	0	0	0	0	0	0	0	
Machico	10	0	0	3,926	1,507	0	2,979	804	
Ponta do Sol	6	0	0	0	0	0	0	0	
Porto Moniz	75	32,217	5,678	6,296	3,564	5,083	0	0	
Porto Santo	40	0	0	0	0	0	0	0	
Ribera Brava	44	0	0	0	0	0	0	0	
Santa Cruz	6	70	0	0	0	0	0	0	
Santana	122	103	20,394	1,987	4,979	4	7	0	
São Vicente	335	426	4,607	32	60	0	0	0	
TOTAL	1,526	32,816	31,142	15,241	11,212	5,105	3,011	804	

Instituto do Vinho do Bordado e do Artesanato da Madeira, IP

GRAPES SOLD FOR MADEIRA WINE - 2008 & 2009 HARVESTS

Kg of grapes	Number of Growers 2008	2009	Kg of grapes	Number of Growers 2008	2009
0 - 500	169	199	5000 - 6000	61	46
500 - 1000	204	234	6000 - 7000	40	38
1000 - 1500	186	183	7000 - 8000	37	36
1500 - 2000	154	121	8000 - 9000	27	24
2000 - 2500	105	100	9000 - 10,000	12	19
2500 - 3000	62	77	10,000 - 15,000	51	38
3000 - 3500	62	60	15,000 - 20,000	23	20
3500 - 4000	43	47	20,000 - 25,000	14	9
4000 - 4500	46	26	25,000 - 30,000	8	1
4500 - 5000		25	30,000 - 35,000	3	0
			35,000 - 40,000	0	1
Total number of growers				1,345	1,304

Instituto do Vinho, do Bordado e do Artesanato da Madeira, I,P

The chart above, shows the number of growers and the weight of grapes sold to the producers. These are shown for ranges of 500kg and 1000kg. However, it is important to highlight the fact that many growers supply only very

Touriga Nacional	Tinta Negra	Complexa	Malvasias	Boal	Verdelho	Sercial	Total production
1,910	0	16,433	116	80,793	23,602	94	127,472
0	2,220,363	13,041	40	35,80	11,323	13,428	2,296,042
0	268	6,475	13	3,003	1,451	278	12,685
12,609	0	993	579	0	100	0	23,507
0	891	0	0	3,195	0	0	4,086
24,364	0	3,635	990	0	13,927	28,298	124,352
0	0	0	0	25	0	0	33,973
0	43,332	268	76	22,892	1,380	1,000	69,627
972	268	1,444	10	1,119	50	0	4,023
18	200	48,967	177,784	60	8,683	3,549	267,688
261	1,577,676	10,246	739	0	13,838	4,510	1,611,879
40,134	3,842,998	101,502	181,226	146,757	73,838	51,157	4,575,334

small amounts of grapes, which is shown in the table below.

Kg of Grapes	Number of Growers	
	2008	2009
0 – 50	5	9
50 – 100	9	10
100 – 200	35	40
200 – 300	44	46
300 – 400	38	51
400 – 500	38	43
500 – 600	52	44
600 – 700	46	52
700 – 800	41	47
800 – 900	45	42
900 – 1000	20	49
Total	373	433

Instituto do Vinho, do Bordado e do Artesanato da Madeira, IP

RECOMMENDED AND AUTHORISED GRAPE VARIETIES FOR MADEIRA WINE

RECOMMENDED

White	Red
Sercial	Tinta Negra
Verdelho	Bastardo
Boal (Malvasia Fina)	Malvasia Cândida Roxa
Malvasia Cândida	Verdelho Tinto
Terrantez	

AUTHORISED

White	Red
Listrão	Complexa
Malvasia de Sâo Jorge	Deliciosa
Caracol	Triunfo
Carão de Moça	Tinto Negro
Moscatel de Málaga	
Malvasia Babosa	
Rio Grande	
Valveirinha	

Production of Madeira and Table wines 2005 - 2009

VITIS VINIFERA GRAPES USED FOR WINEMAKING (KG)

Year	Madeira Wine	Table Wine	Kept by growers	Total
2005	3,635,993	253,801	1,168,732	5,058,526
2006	4,410,693	238,811	709,216	5,358,720
2007	4,107,248	165,065	475,315	4,747,628
2008	4,668,895	184,722	617,174	5,470,791
2009	3,904,278	211,259	459,797	4,575,334

Instituto do Vinho, do Bordado e do Artesanato da Madeira, IP

PRODUCTION OF MADEIRA WINE

Year	Grapes for Madeira Wine (kg)	Wine produced (litres)
2005	3,551,402	3,629,749
2006	4,410,693	4,313,966
2007	4,104,144	4,016,590
2008	4,668,895	4,349,573
2009	3,904,278	3,749,999

Instituto do Vinho, do Bordado e do Artesanato da Madeira, IP

GRAPES FOR MADEIRA WINE (KG)

Year	Malvasia	Boal	Verdelho	Sercial	Terrantez	Other permitted vwarieties	Total
2005	205,209	196,793	43,665	97,886	479	3,007,370	3,551,402
2006	223,477	216,452	35,862	49,442	1,348	3,884,112	4,410,693
2007	197,118	209,004	42,835	54,258	1,454	3,599,475	4,104,144
2008	166,757	217,757	36,910	38,379	1,582	4,207,922	4,668,895
2009	170,827	112,367	35,305	38,220	2,206	3,545,354	3,904,278

Instituto do Vinho, do Bordado e do Artesanato da Madeira, IP

PRODUCTION OF TABLE WINE

Year	Weight (kg)	DOP Madeirense Volume(litres)	IGP Terras Madeirenses Volume(litres)
2005	253,801	136,122	64,508
2006	238,811	127,950	42,390
2007	165,065	98,125	18,400
2008	184,722	107,670	24,041
2009	211,259	125,994	22,321

Instituto do Vinho, do Bordado e do Artesanato da Madeira, IP

Wines lists

HM BORGES, Sucrs, Lda

3-years-old – Dry: Dry. *Medium Dry:*
Medium Dry. *Medium Sweet:*
Medium Sweet. *Sweet:* Sweet.
5-years-old – Dry: Dry. *Medium Dry:*
Medium Dry. *Medium Sweet:*
Medium Sweet. *Sweet:* Sweet.
10-years-old – Dry: Sercial. *Medium
dry:* Verdelho. *Medium Sweet:* Bual.
Sweet: Malmsey.
15-years-old – Dry: Sercial. *Medium
dry* Verdelho. *Medium Sweet:* Bual.
Sweet: Malmsey.

Colheita/Single Harvest

Rich 1995
Sercial 1995
Verdelho 1995
Malmsey 1998

Other Wines

Boal 1977
Sercial 1979
Malmsey solera 1940
40-year-old Malmsey *(produced
to celebrate 500 years of Funchal
as a city)*.

Other Brands

Adega Exportada de Vinhos
 da Madeira
JH Gonçalves
Araújo Henriques

J FARIA & FILHOS, Lda

Blended Madeiras

3-years-old – Dry: Dry. *Medium
Dry:* Medium Dry. *Medium Sweet:*
Medium Sweet. *Sweet:* Sweet
5-years-old – Dry: Dry. *Medium
Dry:* Medium Dry, *Medium Sweet:*
Medium Sweet. *Sweet:* Sweet.
10-years-old – Dry: Dry. *Medium
Dry:* Medium Dry. *Medium Sweet:*
Medium Sweet. *Sweet:* Sweet.

Other Brands

Zarco: Principal markets – Madeira,
Portugal.
Nau Stª Maria: Principal markets –
Madeira.
Pingo Doce: Principal markets –
Madeira, Portugal.

JUSTINO'S, MADEIRA WINES, SA

Blended Madeiras

3-years-old – Dry: Fine Dry. *Medium
dry:* Fine Medium Dry. *Medium
sweet:* Fine Medium Rich. *Sweet:*
Fine Rich
5-years-old – Dry: Reserve Fine Dry.
Medium dry: Reserve Fine Medium
Dry. *Medium sweet:* Reserve
Fine Medium Rich. *Sweet:* Reserve
Fine Rich
10-years-old – Dry: Old Reserve Fine
Dry. *Medium dry:* Old Reserve Fine

Medium Dry. *Medium sweet:*
Old Reserve Fine Medium Rich
Sweet: Old Reserve Fine Rich

Varietal Madeiras
10 Years (Old Reserve) – Dry: Sercial.
Medium dry: Verdelho. *Medium
sweet:* Boal. *Sweet:* Malvasia.

Colheita
Sweet (Rich) 1995, 1996, 1997, 1998.
Sercial 1998
Verdelho 1998
Boal 1998
Malvasia 1998

Terrantez
Old Reserve

Frasqueira (Vintage)
Sercial 1940, 1944
Verdelho 1934, 1954
Bual 1934, 1964, 1978.
Malmsey 1933, 1964.
Terrantez 1978

Other Brands
East India Madeira: Principal markets
– Japan, Poland and Germany
Broadbent: United States and England
(*Reserve Fine Rich and Malmsey 10
Years Old*)
Colombo: Germany and Madeira
Island (*includes the IGP table wines,
red and white*).

**HENRIQUES & HENRIQUES
VINHOS, SA**
3-years-old – Dry: Monte Seco, Special
Dry. *Medium dry:* Medium Dry,
Rainwater. *Medium rich:* Medium
Rich. *Rich:* Full Rich
5-years-old "Reserve" – Dry: Finest
Dry. *Medium dry:* Finest Medium.
Medium rich: Finest Medium. *Rich:*
Finest Full Rich
10-years-old – Dry: Sercial. *Medium
dry:* Verdelho. *Medium rich:* Bual.
Rich: Malmsey
15-years-old – Dry: Sercial. *Medium
dry:* Verdelho. *Medium rich:* Bual.
Rich: Malmsey

Colheita
1995 Sweet (from Tinta Negra)
1998 Sweet (from Tinta Negra)
2000 Boal

Vintage
Malvasia 1954
Sercial 1971, 1964
Verdelho 1934
Boal 1980, 1957, 1954
Malvasia 1954
Century Malmsey 1900

Reserve
Sercial 1965
Grand Old Boal
W.S. Boal
Malvasia 1964

Recent Releases
20 year old Malvasia
2001 Malmsey (*M&S in UK*)

Other Brands
Casa dos Vinhos da Madeira
Carmo Vinhos
Antonio Eduardo Henriques
Veiga
Belem's Madeira Wine Lda.

MADEIRA WINE COMPANY
BLANDY'S
3-years-old – Dry: Duke of Sussex,
  Medium Dry: Rainwater. *Medium*
  Rich: Duke of Cumberland. *Rich:*
  Duke of Clarence Rich.
5-years-old – Dry: Sercial. *Medium*
  Dry: Verdelho. *Medium Rich:* Bual.
  Rich: Malmsey
10-years-old – Dry: Sercial. *Medium*
  Dry: Verdelho. *Medium Rich:* Bual.
  Rich: Malmsey
15-years-old – Medium Rich: Bual.
  Rich: Malmsey

Colheita
Sercial 2001
Verdelho 2000
Bual 1993, 1991
Malmsey 1993, 1990

Other wines
Alvada
Harvest 2004, 2001, 1999

Frasqueira (Vintage)
Sercial 1974,1966, 1962, 1940
Verdelho 1977,1968
Bual 1964, 1959, 1958, 1948, 1920
Malmsey 1985
Terrantez 1976

COSSART GORDON
3-years-old – Dry: Viva. *Medium Dry:*
  Rainwater. *Medium Rich:* Medium
  Rich. *Rich:* Rich
5-years-old – Dry: Sercial. *Medium*
  Dry: Verdelho. *Medium Rich:* Bual.
  Rich: Malmsey
10-years-old – Medium Rich: Bual.
  Rich: Malmsey
15-years-old – Medium Rich: Bual

Colheita
Sercial 1997, 1991
Verdelho 1995,
Bual 1997, 1995
Malmsey 1998,1996.

Other wines
Harvest: Rich 1999.

Frasqueira (Vintage)
Sercial 1960
Verdelho 1975, 1973, 1934
Bual 1976, 1969, 1963, 1958, 1908
Terrantez 1977

LEACOCK'S

3-years-old – Dry: Dry Aperitif.
Medium Dry: Rainwater. *Rich:* Rich
5-years-old – Dry: Sercial. *Medium
Dry:* Verdelho. *Medium Rich:* Bual.
Rich: Malmsey
10-years-old – Medium Rich: Bual
15-years-old – Medium Rich: Bual.
Rich: Malmsey

Frasqueira (Vintage)
Sercial 1963, 1959, 1950
Verdelho 1973
Bual 1966, 1934
Malmsey 1978, 1933

MILES

3-years-old – Dry: Dry. *Medium Dry:*
Rainwater, Medium Dry. *Medium
Rich:* Medium Rich. *Rich:* Rich.
5-years-old – Dry: Dry. *Medium Dry:*
Medium Dry. *Medium Rich:* Medium
Rich. *Rich:* Rich
10-years-old – Rich: Malmsey

PEREIRA D'OLIVEIRA (VINHOS), Lda

3-years-old – Dry: Dry. *Medium
Dry:* Medium Dry. *Medium sweet:*
Medium Sweet. *Sweet:* Sweet
5-years-old – Dry: Dry. *Medium
Dry:* Medium Dry. *Medium sweet:*
Medium Sweet. *Sweet:* Sweet
10-years-old – Dry: Dry. *Medium
Dry:* Medium Dry. *Medium sweet:*
Medium Sweet. *Sweet:* Sweet
15-years-old – Dry: Dry. *Medium
Dry:* Medium Dry. *Medium sweet:*
Medium Sweet. *Sweet:* Sweet

Harvest
Sercial 1989
Verdelho 1981, 1985
Boal 1983, 1984
Malvasia 1989, 1990
Terrantez 1988

Frasqueira (Vintage)
Sercial 1971, 1969, 1937, 1910.
Verdelho 1973, 1966, 1905.
Boal 1978, 1977, 1973, 1968, 1958,
  1922, 1908.
Malvazia 1987, 1907.
Terrantez 1977
Bastardo 1927
Moscatel 1900,1875
*Many more vintage wines are available
  at the lodge.*

VINHOS BARBEITO (MADEIRA), Lda

3-years-old – Dry: Dry. *Medium dry:* Medium Dry. *Medium sweet:* Medium sweet. *Sweet:* Sweet
5-years-old – Dry: Dry. *Medium dry:* Medium Dry. *Medium sweet:* Medium sweet, Boal. *Sweet:* Sweet
5-years-old – Dry: Island Dry. *Medium dry:* Rainwater. *Medium sweet:* Veramar. *Sweet:* Island Rich
10-years-old. – Dry: Sercial. *Medium dry:* Verdelho. *Medium sweet:* Boal. *Sweet:* Malmsey

Single Harvest

1997 – Medium Dry – Tinta Negra – Single Vineyard.
2000 – Medium Dry – Tinta Negra – Single Vineyard.

Single Cask

Boal 1999 Cask 8a+d *(Only available in some wine shops).*
Malvasia 2000 Cask 44a.
Malvasia 2000 Cask 40a.
Malvasia 1994 Casks 276a *(Only available in some wine shops).*
Malvasia 1994 Cask 232C
Colheita 1995 – Cask23 – Medium Sweet – 100% Tinta Negra.

Vintage

Sercial 1978 *(Only available in US and some UK wine shops).*
Sercial 1988
Verdelho 1981, 1978.
Boal 1982, 1978.

Special Wines

Malvasia 20-years-old Lot 7199
Malvasia 30-years-old Special Lot.
VB Lot 2 – Medium Dry Reserve.
Boal 2001 – Casks 48+84

Other Projects

Fortnum & Mason (UK):
Christmas Pudding
Single Cask Malvasia 2000
Single Cask Malvasia 2001

Rare Wine Company (USA) – Historic Series
Charleston Sercial
New Orleans Medium Dry (Old Tinta Negra + Terrantez)
Boston Bual
New York Malmsey
Savannah Verdelho.

Index

Additional credits

I would like to thank the following for permission to use the photographs reproduced in the book which were not taken by me:
MWC: 19; Juan Teixeira: 67 (*top*);
Paulo Olim: 69; Ricky Foyle: 2, 90, 91, 92, 102,103, 174; Jacques Faro da Silva: 153
Mapping Ideas: Maps on pages 14 and 29